Lakeland Gardens

LAKELAND GARDENS

RICHARD BIRD

WARD LOCK

TO LUCY BATTY

ACKNOWLEDGEMENTS

The publishers would like to thank the following for supplying cover photographs for this book: Photos Horticultural Picture Library (front cover), Harry Smith Horticultural Photographic Collection (back cover). All the photographs inside the book were taken by the author.

The line illustrations are by Kevin Jones Associates.

First published in Great Britain in 1994
by Ward Lock Limited, Villiers House,
41–47 Strand, London, WC2N 5JE
A Cassell Imprint

Text filmset by Cambrian Typesetters, Frimley, Surrey

Printed and bound in Hong Kong

CIP data for this book is available upon application to the British Library

ISBN 0 7063 7118 6

CONTENTS

PREFACE

THE LAKE DISTRICT is not noted for its gardens; the fells and the lakes far outshine anything that man has made, but having accepted that, there are a number of quietly interesting gardens, perhaps not quite in the category of Sissinghurst Castle or Hidcote, yet none the less a great pleasure to visit. On the whole these gardens are not overrun by trippers and at times the solitude is such that visitors can wander about them, almost as if they were the owners, with time to admire, but without the necessity of having to attend to their upkeep. The lack of people in many of the gardens allows the visitor to stand back and take a good hard look, perhaps to criticize, perhaps to learn, but above all to enjoy.

One of the most satisfying facts about the Lakeland gardens is that they are all different. There are certain features such as prevalence of rhododendrons or the presence of water that are common to many, but the treatment tends to be interestingly dissimilar in each garden. There is also a great variety in sizes from small back gardens to vast acres, and yet, surprisingly the former are designed in such a way to seem much larger than they really are. Many are an object lesson on how to design a small garden. Another aspect of the variety of the gardens is that the use of plants varies so much: some owners are more interested in herbaceous material, others in alpine plants, while yet others in trees and shrubs. There is something for all types of gardener here.

The fact that so many of them are set in marvellous scenery may be thought distracting to the eye. However, the most skilful of the gardeners have made use of this, creating vistas in which the scenery is framed, or using the fells to contain the garden, as if they were part of the garden themselves, often giving it a feeling of intimacy that could never be achieved with hedges. The fells that tower above Palace How or Rannerdale Cottage, for example, never appear to feel menacing in spite of their size and dominance; they seem to hold the garden in a benevolent embrace.

The shape and the character of the Lake District is never far away from the gardens; rock and water appear in many of them. Nor is nature far away. Not only do the fells peer over the walls and hedges, but the birds and other wildlife make themselves at home amongst the trees and bushes. Very few gardens are without constant birdsong and some, such as Jack Watson's at Holm Crag, can have as many as thirty-two different types of breeding bird present in any one year. Not all of nature's visitors are so welcome however. Some of the most unwelcome, pretty as they are, are the deer which easily scramble or jump over walls and low fences and do an amazing amount of damage. Many a dwarf rose in Cumbria is due to the deer rather than any genetic breeding programme. Of a smaller size, but no less a pest, are the rabbits, and many gardens have to be wired against this marauder who will more than willingly leave the fells for the tasty morsels available in land under cultivation.

To most people the thought of rain is synonymous with the Lake District. Certainly there is rarely the need to water gardens (the dry spells of some recent years have caught even large gardens without adequate hose pipes to deal with the situation), yet there is also a great deal of sunshine and pleasant weather. It frequently happens that if it is raining in one place it may well be dry in another; often even in the next valley. The high rainfall could cause problems for many of the gardens but, fortunately, the majority contain enough stone to keep them free-draining. This, of course, causes problems if there is a drought, as moisture can disappear quickly. This prevalence of water passing through the soil means that nutrients can be quickly leached out. Thus feeding the soil, especially with organic material, is very important. The soil is generally acid, although there are areas of limestone and even some of alkaline sandstone.

The higher parts of the fells can be cruel in the winter, and for that matter also a bit harsh in summer, but it is surprising how warm many of the gardens are. This is mainly due to the warming effects of the Gulf Stream or their position on a south-facing slope. One of the big surprises is how many gardens can support the Chilean fire bush, *Embothrium coccineum*, which most gardeners would consider tender. Its survival is helped by the presence of the conditions it prefers, namely acidic soil, and a moist atmosphere and soil, the latter needing to be free-draining at the same time as being wet. Even quite far inland, at Fellside, near Keswick, for example, it grows very well.

One of the most interesting lessons to be learnt from visiting gardens in the Lake District is that the best way of gardening is to work with nature, rather than against it. Time and again it will be seen that the choice of plants has been dictated by the conditions in which they are to grow. Thus areas of a garden that are wet have been used to grow moisture-loving plants such as rodgersias or ferns. Areas with rocky outcrops have been used for alpines; woodland areas have been embraced and used for the many plants and shrubs that like a bit of shade and protection. In this way the best has been extracted out of every situation.

When visiting these gardens do not expect they will all be the same as when this book was written. Gardens are organic things and are always changing, especially with new plants coming and old ones going. This is due sometimes to the whim of the gardener, sometimes to the effect of the vagaries of weather or of disease in the plants. What is less likely to change is the general feeling and atmosphere of the garden, and it should be the spirit of the description rather than individual plants that should act as a guide to those visiting them.

Opening details

Opening times, entrance fees, road directions and other practical details are given for each garden, and are correct at the time of going to press. Month ranges are inclusive, but if you are making a special journey near the beginning or end of a month, it is worth checking beforehand that the garden will be open. The house attached to the garden is not open unless specified.

Many of the gardens included are private, opened by the generosity of their owners. Although a few of these are open all the time to the public, the majority are open only a few times a year. The latter either open under the National Gardens Scheme, in which case the details can be found in the NGS's annual publication, known colloquially as the Yellow Book, or advertised through local newspapers and noticeboards. NGS gardens usually ask for a small donation to a named charity. Never attempt to visit a private garden at times other than those advertised.

There is much to enjoy in the Lake District. Many of the gardens are well scattered, but since the landscape is such a joy there is little hardship in driving from one to another. May you have as many happy hours looking around these gardens as I have.

R. B.

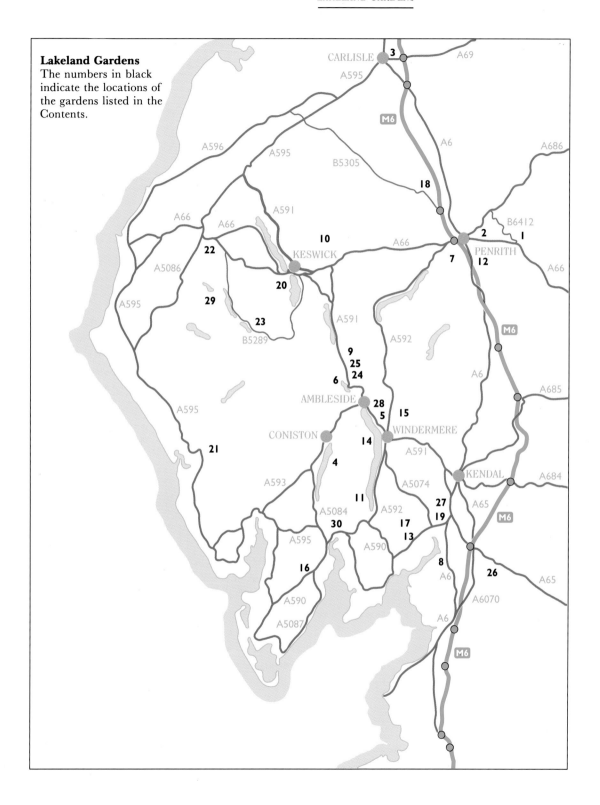

Lakeland Gardens
The numbers in black indicate the locations of the gardens listed in the Contents.

1
ACORN BANK

Temple Sowerby, near Penrith

(Owned by the National Trust)

ACORN BANK is one of the more low-key of the National Trust's properties and there is far less razzmatazz here, with both the garden and its visitors benefiting from it. Situated on the edge of the Lake District, just east of Penrith, it is set amongst fields in gentle rolling hills, where hedges have replaced the more usual dry-stone walls. The main attraction to most people who visit it is the walled herb garden, but there is much more to explore and enjoy in the 1 hectare (2½ acres) of grounds.

The herb garden is a relatively recent creation, but the house and garden go back much further, to 1228 in fact, when the Knights Templar had a religious house there (hence the name of the nearby village: Temple Sowerby). In the sixteenth century the estate came into the hands of the Dalston family and it is from this period that the oldest parts of the house stem. In the early part of the nineteenth century it became the property of the Boazman family and in 1930 it was sold to the writer Dorothy Una Ratcliffe and her husband Noel McGrigor Phillips. Twenty years later she gave it to the National Trust who took over its management in 1969. Unusually for the National Trust it was accepted without any financial backup and so it has always been one of the poorer of their properties.

However, what it lacks in cash it makes up for in charm and interest. Despite the fact that there must have been a garden around the house for centuries, probably both ornamental and productive, it was only the last private owners that have left us anything to look at today, although admittedly the walls probably date back to the seventeenth century when the garden was enclosed by the Dalston family. Much of the current layout and the basis of the plantings is due to Dorothy Una Ratcliffe who also introduced

Open: *end March–beginning Nov, 10–6. £1.40 (free to NT members). House by prior arrangement with lessees (Sue Ryder Foundation).*

Directions: *10 km (6 miles) E of Penrith, on A66 just N of Temple Sowerby. Adequate parking (disabled parking in courtyard).*

Access: *mostly level; woodland walks steep but well maintained. Wheelchair access to main garden only.*

Main attractions: *herb garden, conservatory, orchard, woodland walks.*

Teas: *coffee machine only; Temple Sowerby House Hotel nearby s on A66.*

Plants for sale: *herbs etc from garden; also NT shop.*

Nearby gardens: *Hutton-in-the-Forest (18), Dalemain (7).*

the various pieces of ornamentation such as the spectacular gates and vases from her various travels.

It was, however, the National Trust that introduced the most interesting facet of Acorn Bank: the herb garden. This was conceived by Graham Stuart Thomas, the then garden adviser to the Trust. The former vegetable garden is long and narrow with three beds running down its length. The one on the north side is flanked by a 3 m (10 ft) wall which reflects back quite a lot of heat. The one on the opposite side is, naturally, less sunny and is backed by a lower, 1.2 m (4 ft), wall. The one down the middle is separated from the others by paths and generally receives sun during most of the day except in areas shaded by trees.

The end wall by the entrance is flanked by a greenhouse or conservatory which houses a miscellaneous collection of plants, most of which are considered too tender to be outside. Some are simply attractive, such as the various *Cistus* and the silver-leaved *Convolvulus cneorum* while others, the lemon verbena (*Aloysia triphylla*) and various *Pelargonium*, for example, have scented leaves. Immediately outside the conservatory is a large bed of peonies which contribute the majority of the colour to the garden.

Stretching away from the greenhouse in the three beds is one of the largest collections of herbs in the country, with over 250 species and varieties being represented. Many are culinary, for example costmary (*Balsamita major*), the various mints (*Mentha*) or the onions, such as chives (*Allium schoenoprasum*). Others are medicinal, abscess root (*Polemonium reptans*) or lungwort (*Pulmonaria officinalis*) for example. Some have dual function and can be used as either, thus rosemary (*Rosmarinus officinalis*) can be used in cooking or as a remedy for headaches. Several can be used as vegetables, such as Good King Henry (*Chenopodium bonus-henricus*), for example, which can be eaten as a spinach substitute, or the roots of salsify (*Tragopogon posifolius*). The latter is also known as vegetable oyster after its flavour and it has very attractive purple flowers, making it worth growing for this alone. Many of the herbs have other household uses. Woad (*Isatis tinctoria*) and madder (*Rubia tinctorium*) can be used as dyes, the wormwoods (*Anthemis*) and fleabane (*Pulicaria dysenterica*) help to deter various insects, soapwort (*Saponaria officinalis*) is useful when washing, while the tough prickly leaves of butcher's broom (*Ruscus aculeatus*) can be used to scour the kitchen table. The last-mentioned plant is worth examining in detail as it does not have any leaves at all. Those parts of the plant that resemble leaves are, in fact, flattened parts of stem known as cladodes which serve the same function as leaves. If

Acorn Bank. Herbs may not be particularly impressive as flowering plants but they can have wonderful architectural qualities.

you look closely you will see the small flowers in the middle of each 'leaf' which later in the season produce bright red berries that rival holly for their decorative qualities.

Indeed it is worth taking time to walk round this collection and look closely at all the herbs, many of which are likely to be unfamiliar. It is also worth noting that some plants are poisonous so resist the temptation to nibble anything, just in case you choose the wrong one. Of these the caper spurge (*Euphorbia lathyrus*) is particularly dangerous as the seeds resemble the caper used in cooking. Other poisonous plants include the deceptively pretty Christmas rose (*Helleborus niger*) and belladonna or deadly night-shade (*Atropa belladonna*). Some herbs are neither poisonous nor particularly efficacious. Honesty (*Lunaria annua*), for example, was used to cure lunacy, a state thought to be induced by the moon, as the dried, silvery seed capsules resemble that heavenly body. Lungwort (*Pulmonaria officinalis*) was thought to cure lung ailments as the spotted leaves resemble a diseased lung.

Many hours can be spent in this garden looking at all the familiar names (most are labelled in English and Latin) and the perhaps less familiar plants associated with them. It must be said that herbs do not generally make a very pretty garden. Contrary to popular romantic images, they are often rather straggly, floppy plants and, apart from the green of the leaves, there is very little bright colour in a herb garden, except for the odd touch here and there: the red of the red valerian (*Centranthus ruber*) or the yellow of the yellow flags (*Iris pseudocorus*) for example.

Colour there may not be but herbs come in all shapes and sizes. Some, such as angelica (*Angelica archangelica*) or cardoons (*Cynara cardunculus*), are very statuesque and can hold their place in any flower border. Indeed it may be that in the average garden it is better to mix herbs into an ornamental border rather than trying to create a special area which can become rather dull. However, there are many plants here that would be of interest in any garden. For example there is a large clump of *Veratrum viride* with its wonderful pleated foliage and unusual arms of flowers. Similarly one would be quite happy to grow *Gillenia trifoliata*, *Dictamnus albus* or *Actaea erythrocarpa*, the last especially for its red fruit. Many gardeners will envy the *Daphne mezzereum* that grow here. They are enormous, reaching up to 2 m (7 ft) tall and 2.4 m (8 ft) across, truly magnificent specimens.

Moving through the gateway one comes to a much larger walled garden. This is basically an orchard with mixed borders planted against the walls. The orchard consists mainly of apple trees with an avenue of *Prunus cerasus* 'Rhexii' passing down the centre with the trees lined out on either side of low yew hedges which in turn line the path leading from the house to a gate in the far wall. Most of the apples are old varieties and are labelled. Beneath the trees the grass is left to grow until later in the season so that wild flowers and narcissi can bloom and seed in it. Amongst these are martagon lilies (*Lilium martagon*) which also feature, along with *L. pyrenaicum*, *L. pardalinum*, hostas and foxgloves (*Digitalis purpurea*) in the bed along the south wall which tends to keep quite cool.

Next to the house there are beds of roses of various sorts that will be of interest to most gardeners. One bed specializes particularly in *R. rugosa*, which is nicely underplanted with *Viola cornuta*. Further along, by the steps to the Well Garden are several other interesting species, these being underplanted mainly with *Geranium macrorrhizum*, that doyen of ground covers.

Opposite, at the far end of the orchard and against the north wall, are mixed borders of shrubs and herbaceous plants that carry the seasons through from the spring with *Euphorbia polychroma*, to the autumn with michaelmas daisies, and eventually *Kirengeshoma palmata*. Against the walls are clematis and climbing roses. Unfortunately one section of these borders has been badly affected by honey fungus and has been left fallow until it can be replanted with plants that are not affected by the disease. One cannot but hope that one of the most interesting plants in the garden, which is just opposite this border, does not catch this deadly disease. This is a small tree or large open shrub, the chestnut *Aesculus* × *mutabilis* 'Induta', which is covered in early summer with stubby pink

Acorn Bank. A delightful mixture of *Lilium pyrenaicum*, *Meconopsis cambrica* and hostas.

'candles'. It is a very attractive plant that would do well in a small garden, not casting so much shade (unlike its bigger relations) that it cannot be underplanted.

Leaving the orchard the visitor walks down some steps to the Well Garden which is enclosed on two sides by the house and on the other two by banks. The bank close to the orchard is, as already mentioned, covered with roses, but the other is used as a series of small terraces on which colourful alpines are grown. These include rock roses (*Helianthemum*), saxifrages, *Erinus alpinus*, and a large bush of the bright yellow-flowered *Euryops acreus*. The beds around the walls of the house are mainly filled with bergenias, with clumps of Japanese anemones (*Anemone* × *hybrida*), London pride (*Saxifraga* × *urbium*) and a scattering of Welsh poppies (*Meconopsis cambrica*).

There is a magnificent pair of gates through which you can leave the garden, but it is perhaps better to exit through the smaller gate in the walled garden, which will take you to the top of a path that winds down through the trees to the river and back again. This wild garden is at its best in the spring when it is full of daffodils, but it also contains many other wild flowers and is a pleasant walk at any time of the year. Many of the wild flowers were introduced by Dorothy Una Ratcliffe, who is reputed to have planted 20 000 daffodils here. This sloping garden is covered with mature trees, many of them oak, from which the name of the house, Acorn Bank, is derived.

Another walk has recently been introduced from the car park down to an old watermill that is in the process of being restored. This is more in the way of a nature walk rather than a garden walk, but it is, none the less, an agreeable stroll on a hot afternoon, as it is under trees and skirts the river.

The gardens at Acorn Bank are pleasurable without being overpowering in their brilliance. They have plenty of interesting plants, especially in the herb garden, many of which are not frequently seen in cultivation. It is certainly worth spending half a day here wandering around.

2
BEAUHILL

Beacon Edge, Penrith

(Owned by Mr and Mrs H. C. Barr)

THIS GARDEN, like the next (The Beeches), is run by dedicated plantsmen and it is more than likely that there will be many plants here that the visitor has never seen before. Many plantsmen are only interested in the plants they grow and not in the effect they create and so their gardens become intellectually interesting, but visually rather boring. Beauhill is not like that at all; the visual effect is as exciting as the plants it contains.

The garden is built into a hillside above Penrith, looking south west across the Eden valley towards the Lakeland fells that are spread out before it. It has a natural slope to it, but although it has no natural outcrops of rocks, these have been provided by the Barrs in plenty as their main interest is in alpine plants. However, their interpretation of alpines is broad and there are also plenty of trees, shrubs and perennial plants to be seen.

The garden is well broken up with trees, some of which are quite mature, and along with the shrubs they provide protection and lots of different microclimates, which are essential in a garden with plants of such diverse needs. They are not all grown simply for these purposes; many are attractive in their own right (and may even need the protection supplied by others). Being in the Lake District, the garden has a number of rhododendrons and conifers, but mixed in with them are eucalyptus and phormiums (as many of the plants here are from the southern hemisphere).

Among the exotics featured here is the very attractive *Desfontainea spinosa*, a shrub from Chile and Peru with evergreen leaves, very much like holly, and long tubular scarlet red flowers with a touch of yellow at their mouth. This is relatively tender, but it has obviously found the right place in this garden as it is a thriving bush. Another plant from Chile, this time a climber, that is also rather tender is

Open: *limited (see Yellow Book and local press). Small entrance fee.*

Directions: *outskirts of Penrith. From town centre, follow signs to Beacon Edge. Turn R: Beauhill on L, about 274 m (300 yd) after town limit sign.*

Access: *mostly gentle slopes.*

Main attractions: *alpines, plants from southern hemisphere, especially New Zealand.*

Teas: *teashops in Penrith.*

Plants for sale: *Holden Clough nursery at Holden; Bolton-by-Bowland for range of alpines.*

Nearby gardens: *Hutton-in-the-Forest (18), Dalemain (7), Greencroft House (12).*

Beauhill. Although there are plenty of interesting trees and shrubs in this garden, it is the scree beds that contain some of the most interesting plants.

the rare *Mutisia oligodon*. It can get through most winters as long as it has free drainage and a sunny site, but it does need a warm summer to produce flowers.

Many of the plants at Beauhill are from New Zealand. There has been an increasing interest in plants, especially alpine plants, from this part of the world and a surprising number are now grown in Britain. There are quite a number available in the nursery trade but many more are swapped by gardeners interested in them. There is plenty of seed available both through the seed exchanges, such as those run by the Alpine Garden Society in this country, and through that of the New Zealand Alpine Garden Society, and through other sources within that country. The Barrs have exploited all these avenues and have built up an impressive collection of plants, many probably unique in this country.

When visitors pass along the path that continues from the drive, they pass through an area designed to represent the tussocky hillsides of New Zealand. Here there are several grasses, some stiff, some forming floppy clumps. Amongst these are some flowering plants including a few aciphyllas. These are attractive, but rather vicious plants as the leaves are generally very hard and spiky. They are the kind of plant that gardeners generally refuse to weed under, even if they are wearing gloves. When they bloom they do so in a curious flower spike. Some can be quite big, reaching a few feet (up

18

to a metre); others are small, reaching only an inch or so (a few centimetres) high. Some of the latter can be found on the scree beds elsewhere in the garden.

Moving into the main part of the garden, you will pass the propagating area and alpine house on the way; here there are a large number of beds all linked by grass paths or lawns, except at the lower end where the paths weaving through the beds have been covered with wood shavings. The beds are all different in character. Some of the more recent ones are true scree beds with several inches of gravel or small stones heaped on either the native soil or on an enriched one. Many of the alpine plants that like very good drainage are very much at home in these beds. However, some plants prefer more moisture and there are some beds created where the water naturally drains from the upper part of the garden. In these there is an accumulation of organic material and here the moisture lovers and woodlanders, such as the trilliums and arisaemas, are grown, both represented by a number of species.

There are a number of orchids in the garden including two magnificent slipper orchids: *Cypripedium regina* and *C. calceola*. With similar-shaped flowers to the last, but in no other way

Beauhill. A border reminiscent of the New Zealand hillsides with tussocky grasses and flowering plants from that part of the world.

remotely connected to it, is the small bush of *Jovanella sinclairii* with its purple-spotted white, pouched flowers. This is another New Zealander. One of the Barrs' favourite genera is that of *Celmisia*, with daisy-like flowers, generally over silver or silvery-green foliage. It is surprising how many of the New Zealand plants have white flowers. Generally speaking where a plant would have a blue flower in the northern hemisphere its counterpart in New Zealand will have white (possibly this is related to the evolution of pollinating insects). Thus, although there are typically blue gentians at Beauhill, there is also the New Zealand species *Gentiana saxosa* with its white flowers.

There are far too many interesting plants in this garden to mention them all and to go on would simply produce a catalogue. For anyone wishing to look at a very fine collection of alpine and other rare plants then this is the place to come, while anyone wishing to construct rock gardens or scree beds will find in this garden a very practical object lesson. For those interested in New Zealand plants then this will be their Mecca.

This, then is a garden well worth looking out for, even if it is a little way out from the Lakes. It is especially worth trying to get there when it is open in the spring, although it is interesting at all times of the year.

3
THE BEECHES

Houghton, near Carlisle

(Owned by Mr and Mrs J. B. McKay Black)

THERE ARE NOT many gardens open to the public in the Lake District that can truly be called plantsmen's gardens (this and the previous garden are the only real exceptions). Most make use of a wide but relatively familiar number of plants to create the effects they need. At the Beeches the visitor is guaranteed to see plants that, although they may have read about them, they will not have seen before. It is a plantsman's garden *par excellence*.

As soon as you enter the front gate you are aware that you are in an extraordinary garden. In spring the first thing you are bound to notice is the two round beds of pulsatillas. These, however, are no ordinary pulsatillas. These are semi-double ones, grown from seed imported from a garden in the former Czechoslovakia. They are very exciting plants with flowers a bit like Chinese asters and come in a wonderful range of colours from whites and pinks through to reds and purples. Over the next few years these plants are set to become popular, especially now that the growers in Holland have caught up with them, but for the moment they are in the hands of a select few and nobody has a collection to match this one.

Those with sharp eyes will see that as well as pulsatillas there are the pointed noses of many different hostas beginning to peep through the soil. Later in the year their promise is fulfilled and hostas seem to be everywhere, not only in this small front garden, but in other beds yet to be seen. Altogether there are over seventy different species and hybrids, with more being added all the time. The Blacks are interested in collecting and sowing seed from their own plants, on the chance that nature has produced the ideal cross. From time to time they have been lucky and they have raised some good new forms of hosta.

Ferns are beginning to join the pulsatillas and hostas as favourite

Open: *under National Gardens Scheme (see Yellow Book). £1.*

Directions: *Houghton, near Carlisle. From Junction 44 of M6 take B6264 (signposted Brampton and airport). After 1.5 km (1 mile) turn R to Houghton. Parking in layby opposite shop; The Beeches lies just beyond, on R.*

Access: *level; no problems for wheelchairs.*

Main attractions: *unusual species and hybrids raised from seed, including pulsatillas, hostas, hellebores, alpines and bulbs (most labelled).*

Teas: *Bay Tree tearooms at Border Garden Centre, short way down Longtown exit from M6 roundabout.*

Plants for sale: *no.*

Nearby gardens: *closest is Hutton-in-the-Forest (18).*

plants and a small collection is being built up. Several interesting ones are already flourishing on the left of the house.

One of the most obvious signals that this is a special garden comes from the unconventional, but effective, planting of *Morina longifolia* on either side of the front door. Although its spiky growth and habit make it resemble a thistle, it is more closely allied to the mints, as an examination of its flower will indicate.

There are many other plants to look at in this front garden, but there is even more to see in the various areas at the side and behind the house. Pass through the side gate and yet another obsession becomes apparent, or at least it does if the visitor is early enough in the year, as planted against the wall is a bed of hellebores. It is also here that the Blacks' interest in alpines first manifests itself. Near to the large water pump which dominates this area is a scree bed filled with various campanulas, epimedium, *Salix boydii*, irises, *Mertensia*, several small grasses and many other plants. One of the most dominant is too tall to be considered an alpine. This is the graceful angel's fishing rod, *Dierama pulcherrimum*, here in a wonderful dark rose form, once again grown from seed. On the other side of the

The Beeches. A colourful mixture of alstroemeria, phlox and *Veratrum nigrum* decorate one of the many borders in this garden.

path is a series of stone troughs and sinks, filled with dwarf conifers and other alpines. Behind this is the first of several raised beds, mainly supporting shrubs, but underplanted with bulbs and herbaceous plants such as epimediums and peonies. In the middle of this part of the garden is a damp area where astilbes, primulas, *Caltha* and *Lysichiton* grow. At one end is a very interesting bed of trilliums.

Through a short yew avenue the visitor comes to the main garden. Immediately in front are two long raised beds, running the length of the garden and housing many interesting alpines and bulbs. The architectural backbone of the planting is provided by dwarf conifers, probably one of the best collections in the area. Conifers play a very important part in this garden, providing constant colour and framework throughout the year. At the far end of the right hand bed there is a large outcrop of tufa, a porous rock in which many difficult alpines will eventually grow with relish. This is newly installed, yet already small *Dianthus*, saxifrages, *Geranium farreri* and even a dwarf conifer have settled down well.

The rest of this large part of the garden is taken up with small trees, shrubs and herbaceous plants in borders linked by grass paths. Apart from conifers a genus of trees that is well represented here is that of the rowan or mountain ash, *Sorbus*. These are ideal trees for a small garden as they are attractive in flower in spring, and in leaf and berry in autumn. They also have the advantage of not taking up too much space and of letting sufficient light and moisture reach the ground to allow other plants to be grown right up to their trunks. There are several interesting forms in the garden including the rarely seen *S. fruticosa* and *S. cashmeriana*, grown from the seed of one of the early introductions.

Another genus of plants that interests the Blacks is the diascias, several species of which are scattered around the garden, including some rather interesting hybrids that have occurred. The herbaceous beds are full of all kinds of fascinating plants. There are, for example, a large number of lilies and orchids. Two intriguing groups of plants are the statuesque clumps of *Veratrum nigrum* and *V. viride*, which can be seen in different borders. In their various seasons, bulbs can be seen everywhere in the garden, *Fritillaria*, *Galanthus* and *Erythronium* being especial favourites.

As with most gardens in the Lake District, water is never far away and here it is represented by a pond in one corner of the garden. Nearby is a large damp peat bed brimming with plants that love moist conditions, especially primulas. Rhododendrons, another Lakeland favourite, are also present in quite large numbers. These tend to be mainly the smaller varieties and there is a new planting of yakushimanum hybrids along the far path. Also along this path can be seen groups of the Himalayan blue poppy, *Meconopsis betonicifolia*.

This is a magnificent garden with much to look at and admire. Most plants are labelled; if not Mr and Mrs Black will tell you what they are and willingly answer any questions you may wish to ask. Undoubtedly it is best to visit this garden in spring but, like all good gardens, it still has much to offer throughout the rest of the year.

The Beeches. Alpines are favoured plants in this garden and many gems can be found tucked away amidst the conifers on the raised beds.

4

BRANTWOOD

East Lakeside, Coniston

(Owned by the Brantwood Education Trust)

THE GARDEN at Brantwood, the home of John Ruskin, is not a garden in the conventional sense of a plot of land surrounding the house. Rather it consists of various bits and pieces of cultivated land dotted around the hillside both above and below the house all linked by the natural woodland of the lower fells. Indeed it was the natural woodland that appealed to Ruskin most. He much preferred the tough, but delicate wild flowers of the area to those brash plants more commonly seen in Victorian gardens. Mind you, this attitude did not extend to the bright rhododendrons and azaleas which he planted in abundance around the estate.

Ruskin bought the house and estate in 1871 from W. J. Linton when it consisted of 6.5 hectares (16 acres). By the time Ruskin died he had increased it to 200 hectares (500 acres), about twice the size it is today. W. J. Linton was a keen amateur botanist and while at Brantwood produced a small book entitled *The Ferns of the English Lake District*. In an area of the wood above the ice house volunteers are creating three large beds of ferns dedicated to Linton. The first is a bed of ferns that he found in the Coniston area, the second is to include cultivated varieties that have been developed from these, and the third is a large border of other ferns and their various cultivated forms that Linton found elsewhere in the Lake District. Although still in its infancy this is already a fascinating project and looks set to become a place of pilgrimage for fern lovers.

Ruskin's attitude to gardens was to use whatever was already there. He loved the natural shapes and forms and got a great deal of pleasure by taking visitors onto his hillside garden 'pointing out each trail of ivy and nest of moss, as a gardener of the other species might point out his orchids'. Before Ruskin's time the woods had

Open: mid-March–mid-Nov, 11–5.30. Free. House also open (same times).

Directions: 3 km (2 miles) s of Coniston, on E bank of Coniston Water (follow signs). Also by ferry or NT's steamboat Gondola from Coniston. Ample parking.

Access: hilly but lawn, with magnificent views, accessible by wheelchair.

Main attractions: natural garden, woodland, rhododendrons. Much restoration/construction in progress (fernery, Swiss garden, cottage garden).

Teas: Jumping Jenny tearoom in grounds for excellent lunches and teas (11–6); occasional summer suppers.

Plants for sale: good range and quality.

Nearby gardens: Hilltop (14), Graythwaite (11).

25

been regularly coppiced for charcoal, but he allowed the stools to grow uncut. However, in certain places he deliberately thinned them so that the lake could be seen hazily through them. Throughout the wood he (and the twelve gardeners he brought with him) cut paths, creating steps and bridges where necessary. For the most part these are still discernible and have been gradually restored.

Brantwood. Yellow azaleas planted by John Ruskin against the fell and lake backdrop around his Lakeland home.

Water seemed to have a deep fascination for Ruskin. As well as his love of the ever-present lake he spent a great deal of his time working on one or other of the three streams or becks that flowed through the garden. Being at the whim of the Lakeland weather, none of them flowed constantly. Hence he built reservoirs above the

garden so that he could regulate the flow down the hillside, the streams cascading over the rocks on their way to the lake, creating a continual sound of tumbling water near the house. Over these streams he built bridges that looked as natural as possible.

Much of the water in the reservoirs came from a piece of moorland, way above the main garden, which he drained. He firmly believed in turning waste land into productive use, both to feed the body and for the spiritual satisfaction it produced. He tried various experiments in growing fruit trees as well as the better adapted cranberries and other produce that, should they have succeeded, could be adopted by the poor in the region. This moorland garden has disappeared.

On a more practical level he created a cottage garden in the woods just above the coach house (now the Gallery and the Jumping Jenny bistro). This was known locally as the Professor's Garden and is now under restoration closely following contemporary descriptions. He again filled it with fruit trees (mainly espaliered) and bushes, which he particularly loved to see in blossom, although he was also quite partial to their fruit. He also grew some vegetables and some simple flowers, again, many that would have grown in the surrounding hills. Here he was once more

27

trying to find out what would grow in the barren conditions of a hillside garden so that he could improve the lot of local cottagers.

This small garden is tucked away on the hillside amongst the trees and natural vegetation and can come as a bit of a surprise unless you are expecting it. As with the Linton Garden, the restoration is still in its infancy.

In front of the house there is what would appear to most people as a more conventional garden. Immediately outside the front door is a small lawn on the lake side of which, as the land slopes away to the road, is a large bank of yellow azaleas (*Rhododendron luteum*) which are reputed to have been planted by Ruskin himself. They are at their peak in early summer. These azaleas have been underplanted with shade-loving plants which are at their best just inside the gate with the large clump of Solomon's seal (*Polygonatum* × *hybridum*). In spring there are also primulas and *Cornus canadensis*, and in the autumn *Colchicum speciosum*. From the lawn there are some of the best views in the Lake District. There are a couple of benches here, where it is possible to sit and watch the boats on the lake, and the high fells beyond.

Round on the north side of the house the banks are being turned into a Swiss garden, which will eventually contain plants from that country. Although it is not a very big area the planting is generous with several plants of each variety being planted rather than single ones which can make for a very spotty appearance. This again is a garden still in its infancy, but the prospects look good. Unfortunately it is a bit of an uphill struggle as the local rabbits seem as partial to Swiss plants as mankind is to Swiss chocolate, but doubtless the battle will be won.

It has been won in the herbaceous borders that go down to the landing stage where the National Trust's only boat, the steamboat *Gondola*, unloads the passengers from Coniston, across the Lake. Here rabbits are kept at bay with wire netting which has been attached to the trellising that backs the borders, cleverly hiding the wire as well as giving it support.

John Ruskin firmly believed in using natural flora in his gardens rather than the plants loved by the majority of gardeners. However, he was in sympathy with cottage gardens and it is the effect of this type of planting that has been attempted on the walk down to the lake. On either side of the wide path are mixed borders containing herbaceous perennials and small shrubs mixed together in a whirl of colour. Here are to be seen several old friends such as oriental poppies (*Papaver orientale*), *Iris sibirica*, geraniums, pulmonarias, nasturtiums (*Tropaeolum majus*), *Euphorbia palustris* and *E. characias*, as well as some rarer plants. If you get there early enough (late winter) you will see and smell the winter honeysuckle, *Lonicera* × *purpusii*, which is just inside the top gate. Also in this corner is something that will both surprise and gladden the heart of a Kentishman, namely a large vine of hops which reaches its best in the autumn (somehow this seems a very typical Ruskin plant, one that he would recommend to a cottager). This is an enjoyable border that bids the visitors from the lake a very pleasant welcome.

To the south of these borders is a large patch of rough grass that Ruskin turned into his daffodil meadow. During spring this is a sight to behold — a sea of yellow. It is not planted with the brash modern cultivars (although a few have crept in), but with the much smaller wild daffodil, *Narcissus pseudonarcissus*. This is bordered by a path edged with orange and yellow azaleas, which leads down to Ruskin's harbour.

On the other side of the road where the car park has been built was the site of the glasshouses that used to supply the house with its winter produce. In the car park are two little protruding beds, one containing a collection of bamboos and the other rosemary. Above the rather nice wall that borders the car park is an area that Ruskin tried to turn into his 'Ziggy-zaggy Garden'. This was a secret area where terraces and paths zigzagged up the hillside, with interesting plants and objects at intervals; odd lumps of white quartz can still be seen under the moss for example. This garden has yet to be fully discovered and renovated. However, the visitor can explore the paths above this through the woods on the hillside which are particularly magnificent in late spring and early summer, not only with the fresh young growth, but also with the many rhododendrons and azaleas. Unfortunately many of Ruskin's original plantings of rhododendrons have reverted to their *R. ponticum* rootstock, but new species and varieties have been reintroduced.

This, then, is rather an eccentric garden. It takes a bit of imagination and exploring to discover it. Some areas are still in the process of being restored, or even being created as in the case of the tiny Kilgerran Garden outside the Studio. Other areas such as that immediately outside the house and the herbaceous borders down to the lake are mature. If you bear in mind its unconventional layout, are prepared to explore it, and to appreciate Ruskin's reasoning, it is an exciting garden to visit. It is currently tended by an enthusiastic head gardener and her staff, plus volunteers, without whose invaluable help a lot of the restoration would not be taking place. Between them they are bound to make this one of the most interesting and unusual gardens in the Lake District.

5

BROCKHOLE

Windermere

(Owned by the Lake District National Park)

Open: *April–Sept, 10–5 (10–10 July–Aug). Free but £2 parking.*

Directions: *on A591, halfway between Windermere and Ambleside. Also by boat from Waterhead (Ambleside).*

Access: *easy, despite terraces.*

Main attractions: *herbaceous borders, wild-flower meadow.*

Teas: *teashop/restaurant in house.*

Plants for sale: *Hayes Garden Centre near Ambleside.*

Nearby gardens: *Rydal Mount (25), Holehird (15), Stagshaw (28).*

BROCKHOLE is billed as the Lake District National Park Visitor's Centre and for some reason one imagines that it will turn out to be a Lake District theme park for those who do not want to visit the real thing. Far from it. In spite of its absence from most directories of gardens to visit, once through the reception area, you enter what is possibly one of the best of the larger gardens in Cumbria.

The house was built at the turn of the century and the gardens laid out soon after that by Thomas Mawson who also created Graythwaite. The main garden consists of a series of terraces that drop away from the house. In some respects their linear form is a bit boring to the modern eye, which has got used to individual 'rooms' such as at Sissinghurst and elsewhere. The big disadvantage of long borders as opposed to the smaller enclosed spaces is that it is difficult to impose a character on them. To a certain extent this has been achieved at Brockhole in the more room-shaped spaces to the sides of the main terraces.

There is no point where you can see the whole garden. After you have walked along one terrace you descend to another, which has been hidden and, rather like a Russian doll, you keep expecting the one you are on to be the last, but there always seems to be one more, until at last you can go no further.

The great thing about this garden is the variety of plants. This becomes apparent immediately you pass through the entrance on the long path up to the information centre. Here unfamiliar plants such as *Digitalis ciliata* and the white-flowered, large-leaved *Ribes parviflora* immediately put in an appearance along with others that are perhaps a bit more familiar such as *Primula beesianum* and *Euphorbia palustris*. At the top of the path is a lawn supported by a retaining wall, bringing the grass about level with the eye. With a stroke of genius this lawn has been left to grow wild flowers and so one looks through the soft grasses, as would a worm, to the haze of white daisies (*Leucanthemum vulgare*) and yellow cat's ears (*Hieracium*). The edge of the lawn is mown to the width of a mower to give a neat finish to the grass. There is a small border immediately on top of the wall carrying plants that will accept the dry position such as pinks (*Dianthus*), sedums, and the decorative onion *Allium moly*.

On the other side of the drive to the information centre, against the house, is a wonderful tree: *Cornus kousa chinensis*. During the summer it is absolutely covered with its small green flowers backed by beautiful white bracts, giving the tree a tremendous feeling of serenity. Unfortunately this tree has had to be partially lopped to allow the traffic to pass, but it is still a sight well worth seeking out. Quite close by is another remarkable sight, perhaps not because of its beauty, more because it is there at all. This is the rare *Cupressus cashmeriana*, a tender plant that cannot normally be grown outside in Britain except for very favoured spots.

In fact this is not a very cold garden as it has been designed in such a way that as the frost descends the hill it is deflected by the house and then rolls on past the garden down to the lake. The walls of the terraces also hold a certain amount of heat and slowly release it like gigantic storage heaters, a point worth remembering when gardening in colder areas.

Leaving the cupressus to the left one passes round to the main

Brockhole. The combination of *Campanula lactiflora* 'Loddon Anna' and *Penstemon* 'Flame' is indicative of the good quality of this garden.

Brockhole. Rhododendrons can be dull when out of flower. Here they are enlivened with *Cardiocrinum giganteum* planted amongst them.

terrace which is adjacent to the front of the house. The tea rooms and restaurant open directly onto it and it is a very pleasant place to sit and have refreshments. While sitting there it is difficult to imagine that just over the wall ahead of you is the first of many herbaceous borders because all that can be seen are the trees at the bottom of the garden with Lake Windermere glinting through them. However if you look more closely at the plants in the narrow borders to this terrace you will soon see that the imaginative planting continues.

Up against the house there are several sun-loving hebes, ceanothus and climbers. Dotted amongst these are various interesting plants, some of which come as a bit of a surprise. For example tucked away in a corner between a buttress and a hebe is a large clump of *Tricyrtis formosana*, one of the curiously flowered toad-lilies. These are late-flowering and will give interest, and fascination, to the bed in autumn. At the far end of this bed is a collection of smaller plants including that lovely small viola *V.* 'Haslemere' or 'Nellie Britton' as it is now more correctly called; *Aster tongolensis*, which is a bluish purple daisy with a golden centre and the small goat's beard relative *Aruncus aethusifolius*. Not all plants are small on this corner as there is a large clump of the relatively new spurge *Euphorbia schillingii* and the enormous leaves of *Hosta sieboldiana elegans*. Nearby is the warning as to what can happen if you introduce another spurge, the small *E. cyparissias*, into a border; it runs everywhere.

At either end of the tea terrace are two square gardens each treated differently, but both, again, including common and rarer plants, most of which are labelled. They are both geometric in design, one having its beds outlined in box and the other delineated by paths.

Immediately in front is the first of the herbaceous borders with large clumps of *Macleaya cordata* at each end, one of which has a pale blue iris growing in front of it which goes rather well with the macleaya's glaucous leaves. A yellow Welsh poppy *Meconopsis cambrica* has sown itself rather spectacularly in the blue iris. The rest of the border is taken up with herbaceous plants of various kinds, too numerous to list, backed with climbing roses against the stone walls.

Separated from this border by a path and a row of egg-shaped yews is a lawn that slopes down to a large bed of rhododendrons and azaleas. Being rather dull outside the main flowering season of these shrubs the border has now been enlivened by plantings of astilbes towards the front and those incredible giant lilies *Cardiocrinum giganteum* and *C. yunnanense* peering over the tops of the rhododendrons.

At the north end of the lawn is a flight of steps that leads to other terraces. This and the path leading from it have all kinds of interesting plants tucked away under shrubs, including, at the top of the steps, a fine planting of *Polygonatum verticiliata*, a narrow-leafed form of Solomon's seal. Below the path and bordering onto the lawn is a new bed that contains plants from the Mediterranean and the southern hemisphere. It is dominated to its right by the wonderful Chilean fire bush (*Embothrium coccineum*) which is in full flower in the early summer. Like the embothrium many of the plants in this bed are sun lovers and are marginally on the tender side but they seem to survive the rigours of the Lakeland winter. Many of the New Zealand plants look as though they should be sun drenched, but in fact in the wild they often grow enveloped in mist and low cloud, not too far removed from some of the summers in this area.

Below the lawn the terraces continue one after the other, too numerous to go into in detail. They are mainly filled with herbaceous plants, often with the same plant repeated several times, but doubtless this repetition will be reduced as new plants are introduced. Half way down the terraces is a kitchen garden. This is a large rectangular plot divided into four sections by paths lined with lavender. Each plot has a different emphasis: vegetables, herbs, fruit and cut flowers. Surprisingly this is one of the few gardens in the Lakes where you can see vegetables being grown.

Not only do the terraces move down the hill, but there are also some on either side, radiating out from the house like ripples in a pool. To the south of the main terraces is a large sloping lawn that is left long in early summer so that the wild flowers can be enjoyed. In fact from this spot can also be seen the large area below that is left as a wild flower meadow where over 150 species of flowers and grasses have been recorded. Below the lawn the ground is quite damp and moisture-loving plants such as various rodgersias and primulas have been planted here. This idea of matching the plants to the land, rather than forcing them into what could be a hostile environment, makes very good gardening sense. Further round, the lawn is kept shorter where there are several outcrops of rock surrounded by conifers and heathers. This attempt at a rock garden is perhaps not one of the better features of the garden. The site however is ideal for a rock garden and, if time and money ever allowed, a proper one would be a marvellous addition to the range of plantings.

Just round the corner is a further series of terraces, the best of which is the rose garden. This is not very big, but it is perfect, and could well be adopted by visitors back in their own gardens. The narrow crescent shape could be adapted to fit into most back gardens. The entrance is through an arch of roses and then the emphasis is on small shrub roses. These are not just dotted around, but planted in groups of three or more of each variety. It contains both old and modern varieties. Below this are further terraces of herbaceous plants and shrubs.

Apart from the flower meadow the other outlying part of the garden to be visited is the new arboretum on the other side of the grounds. As yet the trees are still quite small but their interest will increase as the years pass. Curiously this is one of the few gardens in the Lake District not to have a water garden in it in spite of having a large frontage on the shores of Lake Windermere (it would, however, be inappropriate to try and plant this up as a water garden). There is a damper patch just below the lawn that has been allowed to grow wild flowers and a water feature has been tentatively planned for the field just below this area. The thought of a combined stream and rock garden above leading down to a pool is tantalizing as it would be a magnificent feature if it could ever be achieved, and it would certainly complete the attractions of this excellent garden.

All in all this is a wonderful garden to visit and all credit is due to the head gardner and her staff for the way they are handling its development. Many of the old established gardens of the Lake District are being given a new lease of life with young, professionally trained staff keen to make them really worthy of being visited. Brockhole is certainly already one such garden and is likely to be even more so in the future.

6
COPT HOWE

Chapel Stile, Great Langdale

(Owned by Professor R. N. Hazeldine)

An IMPORTANT lesson to be learnt by looking at private gardens is that one of the keynotes of success is enthusiasm. Enthusiasm for gardens, like passions of any sort, can be all consuming and one can soon detect it in a garden where every corner is crammed with plants and where there is evidence that even more odd corners are being drawn into cultivation. Sometimes enthusiasm gives way to fanaticism for one particular type of plant while sometimes, as here, the gardener apparently has an all-abiding passion for all plants, from tall trees down to small alpines. It is difficult to imagine a garden with more plants crammed in than this.

It is quite a large garden, perhaps a couple of acres in extent, but by the time you have walked through it, it may well seem more, as it is created on a hillside and consists of many sloping paths through the trees and bushes.

The approach from the car park is up a long drive which gives some indication of the range of heights to come. This drive is shaded by the heavy leaves of tall sycamores and yet there is a wonderful display of *Geranium macrorrhizum* growing along the top of the bordering dry stone wall. This just shows what this marvellous plant will tolerate and how versatile it is. One plant will quickly clump-up into a colony and can be used in a variety of positions varying from full sun to deep shade as here. It makes an ideal ground cover, wherever it is placed.

On the other side of this drive wall the land drops away steeply to the road below. It is covered with mature trees, predominantly sycamore, but there is sufficient light penetrating to allow the owner to start creating new paths and terraces and it will be interesting to see what develops here.

Another feature of the upper reaches of the drive is the number

Open: *under National Gardens Scheme (see Yellow Book). Small entrance fee.*

Directions: *8 km (5 miles) W of Ambleside. Take B5343 through Chapel Stile – Copt Howe just N of village, on R. Ample parking opposite.*

Access: *steep slopes. Wheelchair access (with difficulty) to house and lawn, but not to garden proper.*

Main attractions: *sink gardens, rhododendrons, woodland walks.*

Teas: *served from house.*

Plants for sale: *large variety from garden.*

Nearby gardens: *Rydal Mount (25), Stagshaw (28), Brockhole (5), Holehird (15).*

of stone troughs that are arranged beside it. These contain a mixture of dwarf conifers and alpines. Indeed these are a feature of the whole garden and they seem to be everywhere. As well as a passion for plants it would seem that the owner has a passion for troughs as these are all original stone ones of various shapes and sizes. With an area of high rainfall such as this, it is essential that they all have drainage holes and that the compost in them is very free-draining, as, along with most plants, alpines detest being waterlogged. The problem comes if there are a few days without rain as then they must be watered before they dry out. Because of the constant flow of water through them they will also need regular feeding as most of the nutrients will be leeched out.

As you walk round the house you come to a small lawn that looks out across the tops of the trees of the garden and also up to the fells above. From this lawn there is access to all parts of the garden along various winding paths. A suggested route is marked out for you. The paths are narrow, often brushing through shrubs. The basic tree cover is either acers or rhododendrons. The eye is assaulted from all directions by the various shades of pink, yellow and purples of the azaleas and rhododendrons. Their brightness could be over-powering, particularly where two clashing colours come together, but the light green and purple foliage of the various acers beautifully tempers their brashness. There are also many other trees and shrubs including *Cornus kousa*, magnolias, eucalyptus and conifers. Along one of the paths are several *Acer palmatum dissectum*, in purple and green, forming wonderfully shaggy humps like colourful hillside sheep.

There are various beds and borders round the lawn and more are to be discovered as you wander through the various levels of the garden. In some there are often plants that you would not normally see together, because they have different water requirements. Here in a wet climate with a free-draining soil they all grow together happily. For example, one of the lower borders contains *Gentiana verna*, *Sisyrinchium striatum* 'Aunt May', hostas, *Prostanthera cuneata*, *Pulsatilla vulgaris* 'Rubra', *Heuchera* 'Palace Purple', a sedum of some sort, *Helleborus argutifolius* and various lilies: an intriguing border well worth pausing to look at. In a nearby trough there is also the rather unusual combination of *Euryops acraeus* and *Ramonda myconi*.

At the bottom of the garden is a small pond that is being planted. (This garden must almost be unique in the Lake District for not having a stream running through it.) Also from the bottom of the garden, there is a route for the 'adventurous' that leads along to the

Copt Howe (*opposite*): A waterfall of gold lights up the close-packed trees in this densely planted garden.

37

already-mentioned sycamore banks that are now being developed.

Primulas of all sorts, including the candelabras such as *P. pulverulenta*, are found throughout the garden. *Aegopodium podagraria* 'Variegata' has been sensibly planted against a path where it can be controlled. This is the variegated ground elder and although it is not supposed to be rampant, you plant it at your peril, unless you have a natural barrier, such as a path, to prevent it spreading far and wide.

There is a nice (accidental?) planting of *Euphorbia griffithii* 'Dixter' with the yellow *Meconopsis cambrica* growing through it. The latter self-sows all over the Lake District and is a wonderful plant for lighting up a dark spot, but it can become a nuisance as its deep tap-root is difficult to get out from the middle of smaller plants. However, in combinations such as this it is delightful. It accidentally occurs with *E.g.* 'Fireglow' in another garden, but 'Dixter' brings more subtlety to the colour combination.

Hostas are planted throughout the garden. They obviously enjoy the moist climate here and will eventually make some extensive clumps.

Plants are generally not labelled, but the friendly owner will be more than willing to help. He will also help you select plants from the large sales table that he provides. Tea and coffee can be bought from the kitchen and it can be very pleasant just sitting on one of the benches overlooking the garden, especially if you have an interesting companion to talk to, when an hour or more can very agreeably disappear. With so many trees and shrubs around, the garden seems a haven for birds and conversation is accompanied by a constant stream of birdsong.

This is an interesting garden that cannot all be taken in at one glance; you have to explore it. It is a garden of levels, one moment you are looking out over the plants, the next moment you are peering up through them. It is one of those gardens that would be magnificent to grow up in, as there are many features to feed the imagination of a child as he or she roams through it.

7

DALEMAIN

Dacre, near Penrith

(Owned by Mr and Mrs R. B. Hasell-McCosh)

THE GARDENS at Dalemain must be some of the oldest in Cumbria. The house and grounds go back to at least 1156 when the de Morville family built the fortified tower. Also in medieval times a great hall was added (still to be seen) and then the house was considerably expanded during the sixteenth century. In 1679 the estate was bought by Sir Edward Hasell and it has remained in the family ever since. The family owe a debt to Sir Edward, not only for providing them with such a fine home over the centuries, but also for the layout of the gardens which includes the long herbaceous border on the terrace and the walled garden. It was he that planted the *Abies cephalonica* at the end of the terrace. However, he cannot lay claim to the knot garden which goes back to Elizabethan times, but at least he did not bow to the fashion of that time and dig it out!

This is calciferous sandstone country, as can be seen by the local stone used as the soft pink facing of house and buildings. So we have moved away from the rhododendrons and azaleas that are so typical of Lakeland gardens, and are now looking at more traditional borders. However, we have not moved away from the Lakeland climate and plants that appreciate the moister weather such as meconopsis and rodgersias still abound. Being inland, away from the immediate influence of the Gulf Stream, the garden is prone to frosts and winter protection is needed for some plants, especially young ones.

As you approach the house and enter the impressive courtyard surrounded by stables and other buildings you can get no impression of what the garden is going to be like; indeed, you are not certain whether there really is a garden there as none of it can be seen. Having paid, you pass through a wall beside the house and

Open: *Easter Sun– beginning Oct, 11.15–5 (closed Fri, Sat). £2.50 (£3.50 to include house).*

Directions: *5 km (3 miles) sw of Penrith, on A592 towards Ullswater. Ample parking.*
Access: *generally flat, except for Lobb's Wood and Wild Garden (steep steps).*

Main attractions: *Elizabethan knot garden, herbaceous borders, woodland, wild-flower meadow*

Teas: *in impressive medieval hall.*

Plants for sale: *large selection*

Nearby gardens: *Hutton-in-the-Forest (18).*

immediately realize that you certainly have come to the right place. To many gardeners this first little courtyard is an absolute delight, to other visitors it is merely a passage to somewhere else and they unfortunately barely seem to give it a glance as they quickly pass through.

It is not a big area, and is completely surrounded by walls and buildings that tend to keep it in shade for most of the day. Quite sensibly, rather than attempting to grow brash coloured flowers, it is planted with foliage plants, which give it a wonderful sense of coolness and tranquillity. There are touches of colour such as the creamy white of the plumes of the rodgersia flowers, the yellow of the spires of the ligularia and the inevitable scattering of yellow *Meconopsis cambrica* that is to be found everywhere in this part of the world. In spite of these touches of colour there is a predominance of cool green. Even the walls are clothed with green with *Hydrangea petiolaris* clinging to some, and a tall lime tree (*Tilia* × *europaea*) overtopping another. Plants contributing to the greenness include *Rodgersia podophylla*, *R. pinnata*, *Polygonatum* × *hybridum*, *Brunnera macrophylla* and *Ligularia przewalkskii*. The small size and its greenness contrasts very well with the size and sunniness of the stableyards through which the visitor has just

Dalemain. The Elizabethan knot garden with its pattern of box hedges and central fountain.

Dalemain. A wonderfully cool and tranquil courtyard, predominantly planted in greens with touches of white and yellow.

come. It is an object lesson in what can be done with those many damp, shady corners that are so often found in town gardens.

One emerges once again into the sunlight, this time to the vast expanse of lawn in front of the house. Apart from some pink china roses planted against the house there is no planting here, just a view across the lawns to the parkland and fields beyond.

Turning the corner of the house one comes to the beginning of the garden proper, with a wide path that stretches down the length of the house and beyond. This is separated from the adjacent field, and eventually the distant fells, by a very deep ha-ha with shrub roses dotted along the top. The planting beside the house is at first a little disappointing, being mainly restricted to the double Jew's mallow, *Kerria japonica* 'Pleniflora', and that doyen of ground covers, *Hypericum calycinum*.

Once past the house, however, one comes to the long herbaceous border planted against an exceedingly high wall. This is full of the typical plants that one would expect to see in such a border: oriental poppies (*Papaver orientale*), the bright scarlet *Lychnis chalcedonica*, the brilliant magenta *Tradescantia* × *andersoniana*, *Campanula persicifolia*, *Geranium ibericum*, verbascums, *Iris sibiricia*, variegated mint and so on. One eye-catching feature is a large clump of *Crambe cordifolia* with its great haze of white flowers in early summer. The border is backed for most of its length by a very high 6 m (20 ft) wall. This is partially clad with climbing roses of various colours and a large *Clematis montana*. The only plant that has managed to completely scale the heights of the wall is a variegated ivy. It has the central and dominant position and perhaps looks slightly out of character with the herbaceous plants below. Towards the far end, the wall is replaced by a low yew hedge before the border terminates at the large *Abies cephalonica* planted by the first of the Hasell family to live here. The border also dates from this period (1680s) and still includes a sundial, dated 1688, that was specially commissioned by Sir Edward Hasell to decorate the terrace.

Turning right at the ancient conifer brings one into the knot garden which predates the tree by about a century. Unfortunately only half of it exists today as one part was removed when the vinery was built against the far wall. The garden consists of a series of small beds surrounded by low box, *Buxus sempervirens*, hedges. The centrepiece is a small lily pond with a fountain. In the spring the beds are lovely with tulips and later in the year a mixture of bedding and herbaceous plants fill them. The larger ones contain agapanthus surrounded by a mixture of pelargoniums. Some beds are devoted to single colour violas. Others contain other low plants such as annual *Limnanthes douglasii*, or taller ones including lilies, meconopsis, *Allium giganteum* and *Nectaroscordum siculum*, or even rose bushes. It is likely that at one time herbs may have been grown in these small beds.

Moving towards the top of the garden there is a long herbaceous border dividing the knot garden from the lawns. During mid summer this has a predominance of orange, particularly towards one end. These oranges include *Lathyrus luteus* 'Aureus', *Hemerocallis*, yellow *Lilium pyrenaicum* and bright orange *Papaver orientalis*. There are also a number of blues to act as a contrast including delphiniums, *Campanula glomerata*, meconopsis and the bright blue of *Cynoglossum nervosum*. There are also some pinks present, including along the front of the border, which is lined with *Geranium endressii* that forms an edging, much in the manner of a low lavender hedge. There is also a rather nice planting of *Symphytum caucasicum* growing next to and through *Rosa glauca*.

Beyond this deep border are two ascending lawns connected by steps. To the right are two wide borders running the length of the lawns with a path between them. On the left is a single border also flanked with a path. The latter border is overhung by tall trees from the bank below and contains large clumps of shade-tolerant plants including *Thermopsis fabacea*, a perennial with lupin-like spikes of yellow flowers in late spring and early summer. There are also large clumps of a veratrum with its very attractive pleated leaves. Also planted here is the *Euphorbia griffithii* 'Fireglow' that one meets everywhere in the Lakes, not surprisingly as it brightens up many a drab wet day. *Smilacina racemosa* is also here in a large patch, a plant that is not seen in the Lake District as frequently as one would expect.

There are many interesting and attractive plants in this part of the garden, particularly the double border which runs from the knot garden to a beautiful arbour built into the stone wall at the far end of the path. This has a wonderful view down the length of the long path along the length of which are rose arches. Dappled shade is created along these long borders by ancient fruit trees. As well as herbaceous plants there are a number of shrubs, in particular old-fashioned roses, as well as climbers on the tall wall, again roses, as well as wisteria and clematis.

Through the middle of the top wall is a door that leads into Lobb's Wood. This is a small wood along the top of the bank that overlooks the Dacre Beck below. It is mainly a wild area and makes a pleasant, particularly on a hot day, short walk through native trees and wild flowers. As in so many of the wooded gardens in the Lake District the trees are alive with birdsong.

Back near the all-dominant *Abies cephalonica*, from which all the various parts of the garden seem to flow, there is a pair of steep stone steps that lead down to the Wild Garden. This is quite a large area of rough grassland, dotted with trees and shrubs, that runs from the main gardens down to the river. There are a couple of areas that have been cleared and in which large colonies of *Mecononopsis grandis* grow. Paths have been mown through the long grass, which is home to many bulbs, including narcissus for the spring and colchicum for the autumn, and wild flowers of which the martagon lilies are some of the most spectacular. The main path down to the summer house at the far end of this garden is lined with fastigiate junipers. Beyond these are fruit trees as well as orna-mental trees and shrubs. Shrubs include *Daphne mezereum*, a golden elm, *Rubus* × *tridel* 'Benenden', rhododendrons and azaleas, and many others. Once the steep steps at the entrance to this garden have been conquered it is a very pleasant place to stroll and watch the river flow pass. Beyond the Wild Garden, in the field that borders onto the ha-ha in front of the terrace, there used to be a landscaped garden, known as the Low Garden, but all is now meadow, except for the fruit trees on the wall of the ha-ha.

Dalemain is a very old garden in which there is much to enjoy. Few of the plants are unusual, but it is the way that they are used that make the individual gardens and borders what they are.

8
DALLAM TOWER

Milnthorpe

(Owned by Brigadier and Mrs C. E. Tryon-Wilson)

Open: *under National Gardens Scheme (see Yellow Book).*

Directions: *11 km (7 miles) s of Kendal. From crossroads in centre of Milnthorpe (on A6), turn w towards Arnside: Dallam Tower is about 1.5 km (1 mile) on L.*

Access: *mostly flat; sloping walk through woods.*

Main attractions: *extensive water gardens, topiary.*

Teas: *at Levens Hall (19) or Wolf House Gallery, Silverdale.*

Plants for sale: *Reginald Kay's nursery, Silverdale.*

Nearby gardens: *Levens Hall (19), Sizergh Castle (27).*

THE IMPRESSION one gets of this garden is one of restrained elegance and simplicity. As you enter the garden there appears little to see, but a large sunken lawn, a drop of some ten feet or so, with an enormous copper beech, which sweeps the grass, in the centre, and a rising bank covered with large trees forming a gigantic backdrop. Slowly the details begin to emerge. Round the rim are small pieces of topiary shaped from yew bushes, a popular feature in many gardens in the Lakes, perhaps inspired by Levens Hall. As the eyes sweep to the right they cannot but be impressed by the large conservatory with its wonderful curved roof.

However, the real pleasure comes once you have spotted the water garden in the far corner of the lawn. This consists of a pond fed by a stream that winds its way through the wood and along the path before falling into the pool. For anyone wanting to create such a feature in their own garden this must be one of the best examples to follow. The watercourse is sinuous without being fussy, the small waterfalls are of just the right size and the planting is restrained and in character with the elegance of the stream.

The first feature that the visitor sees is the pool crouching in the corner of the lawn. This is overhung by some splendid *Acer palmatum*, as well as a small *Magnolia stellata* with its dainty white flowers, fluttering like short ribbons in the wind. The margins of the pool are crowded with a variegated iris, *Caltha palustris*, *Cardamine rhaphanifolia* and two or three drifts of astilbes, all contributing colour at different seasons of the year. The pool and plantings are just the right size and simple without being over- or understated.

The stream that feeds the pool emerges from the depths of the wooded part of the garden down a lively waterfall, the sound of which echoes under the trees and through the bushes. The planting here is delightful with many bushes overhanging the water, while the shiny leaves of a large clump of *Bergenia* repeat the reflections of the water, but this time on land.

It slowly wends its way down to the main path which it then follows to the main pool. Its way is gentle and meandering with small waterfalls which look entirely natural. The planting beside the stream is not continuous, but is concentrated in small pockets with occasional ribbons of plants following the banks for a short distance. Most are typical moisture-loving plants such as primulas and ferns, but there are occasional stunning clumps of plants such as that of the white snake's-head fritillary, *Fritillaria meleagris*.

There is a rock garden that sweeps down the slope of the lawn to meet the stream, almost as if it were itself a tributary. This has many interesting plants on it including a large clump of *Trillium chloropetalum* in its purple form.

The stream enters the pool over an unseen waterfall, covered by low shrubs. On the other side of the path to the pool, against the wall, is a bed of peonies, fronted by a low retaining wall covered in *Aubrieta* and *Arabis*. All along this path there is a low balustrade in

Dallam Tower. The natural-looking water feature of this garden makes it well worth a visit.

front of the buildings on which are perched at regular intervals old stone troughs containing small plants.

Following the path away from the house the visitor passes into the wood crossing the stream by a delightful Japanese-style bridge. The Japanese theme is continued with a Japanese lantern in a small dell with steps leading from it which merge into the rock garden mentioned above. The result when coming down the rock is somewhat akin to walking on a limestone pavement.

At the top of the slope is another path that runs along through the woods above the lawn. This path is through an avenue of what must be some of the tallest yews in the country. Under these flourish in vast quantities the wild garlic, *Allium ursinum*, which during the late spring can look extremely attractive with their white balls of starry flowers set off against the wide green leaves, but their smell can be overpowering. There are occasional strong clumps of *Rodgersia podophylla* rising from the lower vegetation to take the eye. The wide path brings the visitor back to the lawn along the top of the right-hand bank which includes a rose garden as well as more yew topiary.

Dallam Tower. An impressive feature of this garden is the conservatory surrounded with yew topiary.

This is not a big garden and is certainly not prone to mass planting (except for the wild garlic, but that is nature's doing), and yet it is one well worth visiting if only to look at the way the stream and pool have been constructed and planted.

9

DOVE COTTAGE

Grasmere

(Owned by the Wordsworth Trust)

T HE GARDEN at Dove Cottage is not one of the greatest in the
Lake District. However, it is interesting, especially when taken
along with the one at Rydal Mount, as it is one of the two gardens
that William Wordsworth, the poet, created. In fact, although he
designed and made the garden at Rydal Mount, the one here at
Dove Cottage was more of a joint effort with his sister, Dorothy.

Wordsworth and his sister moved into Dove Cottage in 1799 and
lived there until 1808, during which time, in spite of ill health, they
were blissfully happy. The garden played as important a part as the
house and right from the day they moved in they were constantly
working on it. Both were deeply attached to nature and the
countryside and so one of the two main elements of their garden
was that it should be as natural as possible (plants were for
complementing rather than adorning), being mainly stocked with
wild flowers. The other element was one that was true of all cottage
gardens: it should be productive in terms of vegetables and fruit.

The cottage had once been an inn, the Dove and Olive Branch,
and is from this that the modern name of Dove Cottage is derived.
In the Wordsworths' time it was known as Town End, the name of
the hamlet on the outskirts of Grasmere. In those days the main
Ambleside to Keswick road went past the door and it was quite a
busy thoroughfare, with travellers and beggars often stopping to
obtain what they could. William and Dorothy constructed a wall of
upright stones in front of their cottage to separate themselves from
the road and here created their flower garden. It was mainly
devoted to wild flowers that they collected on their almost daily
walks: primroses, orchids, ferns, mosses, foxgloves, kingcups and
many others.

A small piece of garden is still in cultivation in the front, a patch

Open: *(only in tandem
with house): 9.30–5.30
(or dusk if earlier) £3.50
(includes entry to
Wordsworth Museum);
discount for visitors from
Rydal Mount (25).*

Directions: *just off A591
as it passes Grasmere.
Car park on main road.*

Access: *steep grass paths
in rear garden.*

Main attractions:
*historic connections, the
Wordsworths' orchard,
miniature porchtop garden.*

Teas: *in café beside
car park; or teashops in
Grasmere.*

Plants for sale: *no.*

Nearby gardens:
*Rydal Mount (25).
Rydal Hall (24).*

that leads up to the front door. This contains a delightful mixture of old cottage flowers, still including pansies and foxgloves, also aquilegias, honesty (*Lunaria annua*), bleeding hearts (*Dicentra formosana*), antirrhinums, campanulas, sweet williams (*Dianthus barbatus*), lupins and of course the ubiquitous *Meconopsis cambrica*. The walls of this corner of the house are clothed in roses, *Clematis montana*, *Kerria japonica* and that wonderful everlasting pea, *Lathyrus grandiflorus*. In the Wordsworths' time honeysuckle was introduced as a climber, and in particular Dorothy grew it up yew. On the side of the house she also grew so many 'scarlet beans', runner beans, that the cottage was 'covered all over with scarlet flowers and green leaves'. We tend to forget how decorative these beans are, and their relegation to the vegetable garden can be the flower garden's loss.

The vegetable garden no longer exists, but it was a very important part of their household economy. Within days of moving in they had started preparing the ground and planting. Peas were of particular importance to them and they always grew sufficient to give some away: turnips, broccoli, French beans, kidney beans and spinach were also grown. There are many references to the

Dove Cottage. The small border of pretty cottage-garden flowers by the entrance to Wordsworth's cottage.

vegetable garden in Dorothy Wordsworth's journals and the amount of time they spent working there.

Dove Cottage. The walls of this typical Lakeland cottage form a vertical garden as they are covered with roses, everlasting peas and many other climbers.

There are also numerous references to the orchard, which is at the back of the house and served as much as a lawn and somewhere to sit as to produce plums and other fruit. This steep garden is still there and it is possible to walk around it and feel the atmosphere of the garden. Obviously after two hundred years it is not the same but the general feel is probably similar. Basically it is just a slice of the fellside, mainly down to grass with a few shrubs and mature trees. Here and there are wild flowers. Again these are quite likely to be descendants of the plants originally introduced of which there is ample evidence in Dorothy's journals and letters. Any planting was to enhance the natural setting rather than to decorate it. The one area that was planted more than anywhere else was around their well, which seemed to be more of a spring or small stream than a deep well. Here in the damp they planted kingcups, primroses, ragged robin and red campion amongst other things.

At the top of the garden is a rustic summerhouse in which Wordsworth use to rest and occasionally write poetry. It still has a good view through the trees of Grasmere, although it was probably more visible in his day. They would often sit or lie on the grass under the trees or sit on the rocks that protrude through the soil in natural outcrops.

Today, along the side of the house, there is a fine collection of

Lilium pyrenaicum (a good cottage garden plant) attractively mixed with the sensitive fern, *Onoclea sensibilis.* Another planting that is well worth looking at is that on the roof of the porch to the back door. This is covered with hostas, ferns of various sorts, yellow archangel (*Lamium galeobdolon*), red campion (*Silene dioica*), herb robert (*Geranium robertianum*) and bistort (*Persicaria bistorta*). It is worth visting Dove Cottage just to see this miniature garden, which is simply growing in the moss and detritus on the tiles of the porch. Without the Lakeland's moist climate it would be impossible to achieve this.

That Wordsworth and his sister loved the garden can be in no doubt. In 1802, while still living there, he wrote a poem of farewell to the garden as he set off for two months on one of his trips in which he tenderly referred to it as:

> Sweet garden-orchard, eminently fair,
> The loveliest spot that man hath ever found.

Alas, the poem is too long to include here but it clearly sets out his attitude towards not only this garden but gardens in general.

After Wordsworth's marriage the cottage became too small and they had to move to a larger house in Grasmere. However, he retained the lease for some years and sublet it to a friend, Thomas de Quincey, who lived there until 1830. Dorothy missed it a great deal and, until they moved to Rydal and created a garden there, continued to go back to stand or sit in their old garden. Many a modern gardener would wonder what they saw there, but many others standing under the ancient fruit trees or sitting in the summerhouse further up the hill will understand the attachment that such a simple garden can create.

Dove Cottage. The roof of the porch over the back door contains a miniature garden with many plants including hostas, ferns and bistort.

50

10
FELLSIDE

Millbeck, near Keswick

(Owned by Mr and Mrs C. D. Collins)

THERE ARE very few, if any gardens in the Lake District that are created on flat land, but by comparison Fellside makes all the others look as though they were built on a billiard table. It rises steeply from the road to reach dizzy heights above the house, where, from a clearing, there is a wonderful view of the fells and Derwent Water.

This is an incredible garden and one of which the owners can feel justifiably proud. Where and how you could start gardening on such a slope is a mystery, but Mr and Mrs Collins have gradually tamed this hillside until they have a very beautiful garden extending over 0.4 hectare (1 acre) of ground. It is basically a garden of trees and shrubs through which paths cross and recross each other.

You enter the garden from the road into a tunnel of vegetation and immediately start climbing. The tunnel continues, occasionally breaking into the light, zigzagging up the hillside, past the house. The path is just wide enough for one person to walk comfortably, occasionally brushing a shrub where it narrows. From the top of the garden the path descends into a gully with a stream passing through it before climbing again, only to descend and recross the stream before zigzagging back to the starting place. The whole journey is one of adventure and there is no doubt that at times you could imagine that you are in the Himalayas, especially on the valley section.

Of course there is much more to see than just the path and the views. The garden is full of interesting trees and shrubs. Many of the mature trees, oaks and pine, are indigenous but most of the shrubs have been added. The main emphasis is on rhododendrons of which there are 100 species and 200 cultivars. In many specialist

Open: *under National Gardens Scheme (see Yellow Book). Small entrance fee.*

Directions: *3 km (2 miles) N of Keswick. From A591 turn R to Millbeck, then R at next T-junction. Fellside a short distance on L. Park on verge.*

Access: *very steep terraces and slopes.*

Main attractions: *rhododendrons; steeply sloping garden; views.*

Teas: *The Old Sawmill, Dod Wood; or ask Mr & Mrs Collins for a recommendation.*

Plants for sale: *Lingholm (20), on nearby Derwent Water, has a range of rhododendrons.*

Nearby gardens: *Lingholm (20).*

Fellside. *Embothrium coccineum* grows in many gardens in the Lake District and can be seen to advantage at Fellside.

gardens the cultivars and species are kept separate, but here they are mixed. One reason for this is that the species tend to flower earlier and therefore if mixed the flowering is spread throughout the garden. This is especially important if a late frost knocks out the early-flowering species. Secondly the leaves of the species tend to be more interesting and, again it is useful to spread this attribute around, rather then concentrate it in one area.

To the left of the first turn of the path is a tall tree of *Embothrium coccineum*, the Chilean fire bush. At the time when this garden is open it is in its full fiery magnificence. On the other side of the path scrambling up through some lawson cypresses (*Chamaecyparis lawsoniana*) is *Tropaeolum speciosum*. Like the embothrium this plant is another South American, but will not come into flower until later in the season. This is not a difficult nasturtium to grow and as can be seen here it will grow in surprisingly dry conditions, even under coniferous trees. The path wends its way up past the house with occasional herbaceous plants on the way. On one of the bends above the house is a wonderful tree peony, *Paeonia suffruticosa*, with flowers the size of dinner plates. On another corner there is a classic planting of *Bergenia* (their shining green leaves define a corner well and they have been used in this position since Gertrude Jekyll's time). Nearby, on the top path there is a couple of plantings of *Romneya coulteri*, their silvery leaves seeming a little out of character in this wooded garden. Alas they are not in flower when the garden is usually open.

It is from the top path, looking out over the roof of the house, that the magnificent views can be seen. This area is kept open and with more light plants such as the iris thrive. Further along the going gets a little bit more difficult, with some of the steps being worn. There is nothing wrong with this as it is very much in character with the garden, but it is mentioned as a warning for the less agile, especially as the path is steep in this area. Most of the recent planting has taken place here with rotted bark being added to the soil to help establish the new plants which include a *Fothergilla major* as well as several more rhododendrons.

When the small valley is entered the adventure really begins and the up and down of the path through the rhododendrons and azaleas must make this the nearest you can get to the Himalayas without actually going there. Fortunately at this point there are a couple of seats which are not only welcome for those who wish to catch their breath, but also for those who wish to sit and admire this beautiful valley with its stream gently tinkling its way to the bottom of the garden. The path eventually goes back onto the main slope of the garden and then makes its way back to the front gate.

Being on a hillside the soil tends to be very free-draining, but with a high rainfall this is of no problem except for the leaching of nutrients from the soil. However, on the whole Mr Collins does not feed, except when making the initial planting, when organic material is added, and an annual feed for the camellias. In spite of the high rainfall in this area it is still necessary to water at times, especially for new plantings, so scattered around the garden are watering points which avoid the necessity to carry water up and down these steep slopes. Frost is generally not a problem and relatively tender plants such as the various ceanothus and the embothrium seem to survive and flower well.

This is a most enjoyable garden, especially if you appreciate rhododendrons. Most are discreetly labelled so there is much to learn as well as to enjoy. Mr Collins will also most willingly answer questions about the plants. It is strongly to be recommended that when you emerge from the undergrowth near the gate you turn sharp right and go round at least once more as you are bound to miss things on the first time round.

For anyone with a garden on a hillside this is an object lesson on how to cope with it. The skilful use of paths and the way they have been constructed, often terracing the hillside with logs, shows what can be done with this type of difficult terrain. Not everybody would want to plant so many shrubs perhaps, but there is still plenty to be learnt. For visitors it is a privilege to see such an intimate and wonderfully romantic garden and, from their chatter on leaving, one that they all seem to enjoy.

11
GRAYTHWAITE HALL
near Newby Bridge

(Owned by Mr M. C. R. Sandys)

Open: *April–June, 10–6. £2.*

Directions: *w side of Lake Windermere, 6.5 km (4 miles) N of Newby Bridge on Newby–Hawkshead road. Ample parking.*

Access: *not difficult, despite sloping terrain. A circuitous route avoids steps and makes wheelchair visits possible.*

Main attractions: *rhododendrons, streamside planting, Dutch garden.*

Teas: *teashops in Hawkshead.*

Plants for sale: *interesting range of traditional perennials and shrubs at T. H. Baker's nursery (just s of Haverthwaite on B5278). Also Muncaster Castle (21) for rhododendrons.*

Nearby gardens: *Hill Top (14), Brantwood (4).*

THE GARDENS at Graythwaite Hall tend to be quiet and reflective, making them a joy to visit. They are on a grand scale, but are not overwhelming in spite of some large plantings of rhododendrons for which the garden is justly famous. The predominance of these plants means that the garden is only open during their flowering season, from the beginning of April until the end of June.

The house, which is not open to the public, was started around about 1500 and finished in the eighteenth century. During the nineteenth century the house was 'restored' by refacing it, changing it from a typical Lakeland house to one that was more in keeping with Victorian tastes. Around the time that this work was being carried out, Thomas Mawson was commissioned to lay out the gardens. Mawson was a nurseryman from Windermere and this was his first major commission, one that was to prove a turning point in his life as he went on to design gardens not only in Britain but in Europe and Canada as well. At Graythwaite he adopted a style that was in essence to remain with him. He liked to link the house with the garden and did so with a terrace leading to large lawns and thence to woods or perhaps a more distant view. He worked on the gardens from 1889 until 1896 and they have basically remained the same ever since.

The garden extends to 2.4 hectares (6 acres) of which the majority lie in front of the house and its terraces. However, there is one, almost secret, area that leads off the courtyard behind the house. This is the Dutch Garden. It is a rectangular garden enclosed with yew hedges and dominated in the centre by a tall columnar sundial. The garden itself consists of a number of geometric-shaped beds surrounded by low box hedges. The beds are filled with primulas in the early part of the year. One of the most noticeable features is the double row of yew spheres, each comprising two specimens so that the top half of the globe is golden and the bottom half the normal green, giving the garden a sunny effect even when the weather is overcast, as it often is in this area.

On the house side of this garden are a couple of small terraces planted mainly with shrubs such as rhododendrons, viburnums (including the form of *V.* × *burkwoodii* known as 'Chenaultii'), *Pieris*, *Magnolia stellata* and acers, as well as herbaceous plants including hemerocallis, peonies, hostas and meconopsis.

Going back into the yard, the visitor enters the garden proper through a most splendid iron gateway, well set off by a honeysuckle. It is not long before it becomes apparent that the few rhododendrons in the terrace below the Dutch Garden were but a foretaste of what lies ahead. The path sweeps round through rhododendrons to the end of a terrace that overlooks an enclosed lawn with a small herbaceous border around the edge and a rose garden towards the house end. Both are usually at their peak when the garden is closed to visitors but, unless the voracious rabbits have caused havoc, they are already putting on a display before it shuts its gates at the end of June.

On the retaining walls of some parts of the terraces grow plants

Graythwaite Hall. The Dutch Garden at Graythwaite is a small enclosed area that is in direct contrast to the rest of the garden.

such as *Abutilon* and *Ceanothus dentatus*, which one would imagine were far too tender to grow here and yet they happily survive and flower well.

From the terraces or from the lawn the rest of the garden can be seen as if arranged in a panorama around the blurred edges of the main lawn. To the right rises a hill of choice rhododendrons. During April and May this is a beautiful sight and it is worth sitting a few moments and contemplating it before moving closer to examine the individual shrubs. As the eye continues to sweep around the lawn's horizon it passes the pool beside which is a croquet lawn, the only flat area of grass in the garden, overtowered by enormous beech trees; then on to more and more rhododendrons, culminating in a tall bank of them on the other side of the house, separated from the lawn by a castellated yew hedge.

Graythwaite Hall.
This garden is full of magnificent displays of rhododendrons, which can be seen either in long distance views or in close-up along paths.

What cannot be seen from this position is the lively stream that runs on the west side of the lawn, although its course can be identified by the lush vegetation that runs beside it. Although this appears to be a natural stream it was originally engineered by Mawson. The planting along its length is really marvellous and for

those not so keen on rhododendrons it will be the highlight of the garden. Although it is planted all along its course, often with overhanging rhododendrons, there are large pockets of moisture-loving plants. One of the first, near the steps at the end of the upper terrace is a wonderful planting of candelabra primulas of several sorts and blue meconopsis. Not all plants are so small: gunnera (*G. manicata*) and skunk cabbage (*Lysichiton americanus*) both produce their enormous leaves in a very attractive area below the next bridge downstream. The stream eventually makes its way into a large pool beside which is a new bog garden full of hostas, candelabra primulas, *Iris sibirica*, astilbes and meconopsis. Near the pool are planted a number of *Rhododendron luteum*, the ubiquitous yellow azalea, which perfumes the air delightfully. From the pool you can appreciate the delightful view under the trees back towards the house.

Graythwaite Hall. A well-planted stream runs the length of the garden. Although originally constructed, it has now merged with the natural landscape.

There are several possible routes around the garden when one leaves the terrace: you can either follow the stream or cross it to ascend the hill amongst the rhododendrons. It is interesting to note how well all the rhododendrons in this area have been mulched with grass cuttings and any other organic material going. This is not only helps to keep the roots moist and cool, but provides essential nutrients which are often leached out in the Lakeland's high rainfall. This path will take you past a circular enclosure in which the family dogs have been buried. The path emerges into a large meadow-like area which is used to grow wild flowers and narcissus. Around this are one or two stately specimen trees which are not only clearly labelled with their name, but also the precise date of planting so that you can get some idea of their rate of growth. Among these are a cedar of Lebanon (*Cedrus libani*) planted in 1951, which has put on surprisingly little growth over the last forty years, a tulip tree (*Liriodendron tulipifera*) with leaves that look as though they have had the ends cut off, *Fagus sylvatica* var. *heterophyllus* 'Aspleniifolius' with its wonderful cut leaves, and *Aesculus × carnea* (previously *A. × rubricundra* when it was planted in 1914). A walk round the meadow will bring you back to the pool at the bottom of the stream.

Another route, or a continuation of the previous one, would be to cross the lawn and go into the vast area of rhododendrons. When walking through them the large rounded bushes seem to gather round as if you were walking through towering cumulus clouds. This path leads round to the car park or you can branch off along the drive next to the castellated yew hedge that runs round the edge of the lawn. Through the yew, as in so many gardens in the Lake District, grows the flaming red *Tropaeolum speciosum*, one of the few plants to be trusted to grow through such a hedge. At the far end of this, almost next to the houses is a large outcrop of rock, on the top of which grows a pinkish purple rhododendron and over its face an enormous spread of *Senecio greyi* (now more correctly called *Brachyglottis greyi*). The combination of the flowers of the rhododendron and the silvery grey leaf of the senecio, plus the grey of the rock makes a superb picture. It is only hoped that the rhododendron will have ceased flowering before the yellow daisies of the senecio appear. The path leads past the house and back to the courtyard.

Back in the car park it is worth just looking at the walls as there are several interesting roses as well as *Clematis alpina* 'Frances Rivis'; the wonderfully long-flowering *Solanum crispum* 'Glasnevin', and *Cytisus battandieri* with its small lupin-like tufts of yellow flowers.

The large lawn with odd clumps of rhododendrons dotted around it gives a feeling of great spaciousness as it slopes away in all directions, inevitably leading the eye to various parts of the garden as it disappears between bushes and under trees. It is a very restful, placid garden, one to stroll and sit in rather than rush through. There are rarely many visitors at any one time and so the peace is enhanced.

12

GREENCROFT HOUSE

Great Strickland, near Penrith

(Owned by Mr and Mrs W. Irving)

THIS IS A MOST delightful garden and the fact that it lies a little bit out of what is usually considered the Lake District should deter no one from visiting it. Greencroft House has not got a very big garden, but because it is broken down into a whole series (over a dozen) of individual gardens and areas it seems enormous. It is a garden to visit both for pleasure and for instruction as it is impossible to imagine that anyone can come away from it without being inspired in some way to improve their own garden, both in terms of layout and of plantings.

The Irvings have lived here for over twenty years during which time the garden has gradually evolved from a wilderness. With it has evolved their knowledge and understanding of plants.

The breaking up of a garden into lots of smaller ones is very prevalent today. However pleasant this may be, there is little point (other than creating a wind break) in doing this if you are going to repeat the same kind of planting in each, or giving each the same character. Greencroft House demonstrates perfectly the ideal use of different gardens. There seem to be innumerable rooms, each different in shape, different in plantings, and probably more importantly, different in atmosphere.

As you enter the drive the first intimation that you are in a special garden where every scrap of ground counts, is the semicircular rock bed, making use of an area where a wall was moved. This has quite a number of interesting rock plants in it, none more so than the rare *Morina alba*, which Mrs Irving grew from seed. This is a bit in the manner of *M. nepalensis*, with narrow leaves, fringed with spines and small whorls of tubular flowers that are white in this species. Other plants include the yellow, starry-flowered *Bulbinella hookeri*, *Geranium polyanthes*, and a splendid

Open: to private parties or by appointment only.

Directions: 11 km (7 miles) s of Penrith. Leave A6 just s of Hackthorpe, signposted Great Strickland. Parking beside road and, with permission from landlord, in pub car park.

Access: level and easy-going.

Main attractions: 'garden rooms', colour-coordinated plantings, shade garden, woodland, stream and water garden.

Teas: provided in garden.

Plants for sale: excellent plant stall on open days. Larch Cottage nursery at Melkinthorpe (also has tearoom).

Nearby gardens: Hutton-in-the-Forest (18), Dalemain (7), Beauhill (2).

Greencroft House.
There are many beautiful borders in this garden, several devoted to particular colours. This is part of the hot-coloured border.

Euryops acreus. This bed is a foretaste of what lies through the gateway in a courtyard in front of some outhouses.

Here there are several more rock gardens, each built up from the level ground, rather than making use of a natural slope. The plants used here are far too numerous to mention but a few. Even in summer there is plenty of colour about with *Crepis incana*, a much under-rated pink dandelion, *Zauschneria californica* (now strictly speaking *Epilobium canum*) with soft green leaves and orange tubular flowers, which contrasts well with the soft blue of *Jasione heldreichii*, and *Silene schafta*, a dwarf, dark rose pink campion that is invaluable in the summer with its carpet of flowers. Dotted around here and there are various forms of alpine poppies, *Papaver alpinum*, in different soft colours.

Poppies are obviously a favourite at Greencroft House and moving through into the next area, the herb garden, they can be seen in superabundance in the round central bed. Here the vibrant jumble of bright reds and oranges (the latter of *Eschscholzia californica*) brings gaiety to an area which in some gardens can be a dull place (herbs so often have small, insignificant flowers). In the beds a mixture of culinary herbs are edged with chives and strawberries along the narrow paths. This garden is protected by surrounding trees and shrubs which are not so large that they cut out the light which is so essential to most herbs.

Going back to the drive the visitor passes through soft pink sandstone gateposts into the garden proper. At first it seems to be more of the same with a small rock garden that includes a good plant of the recently intoduced *Penstemon pinifolius* 'Mersea Yellow' and another good plant of *Crepis incana*. However beyond this, starting from a pond, the plants increase in size as the main bed sweeps round the front lawn as a full scale mixed border. The pond is quite a key feature as from it emanates a small stream that runs the full length of the bed, disappearing through the rose hedge at the end. The border is mixed in such a way that there is always something of interest throughout the year, a principle that runs throughout the garden. Hellebores and bergenias start off the year which is then colourful right through until the frosts finish off the fuchsias and other late flowerers. This border is a mixture of shrubs, which are mainly beyond the stream, and perennials in front. In mid summer there tends to be a strong thread of purple and reds in this border as astilbes, penstemon and hebes draw the eye. As well as flowering plants there is plenty of foliage to give the borders substance, from the hostas that decorate the front of the border to the giant leaves of the *Gunnera manicata* beyond the pond. (In mid summer the gunnera is brilliantly set off with the soft billowing flowers of the *Cotinus coggygria*).

Greencroft House. A close up of part of the hot-coloured border. These are difficult colours to combine so successfully as in this garden.

At the far end of the lawn there is a long rose hedge (*Rosa* 'Nevada') underplanted with small pinks. Through this hedge is a narrow garden that is mainly filled with dwarf conifers, but also contains heathers and dwarf rhododendrons. Apart from the spring this is mainly a green garden, a good contrast with a cooling effect after the foregoing borders, emphasized by being fairly small and quiet. At the far end is a small corner, hidden by some larger conifers where colour suddenly erupts in the form of bright astilbes around a pool that terminates the stream that had started in the previous garden.

Beyond the conifer garden is another drive and beyond it a woodland garden containing pulmonaria, hostas, primulas and other plants that like these conditions. The stream re-emerges and follows the path until it finally sinks into another pond, this time under old fruit trees planted in an area of lawn into which the woodland garden merges. This is one of the high spots of the garden (of which there are many). Fortunately there is a bench on which one can sit, as the planting round this pond is truly magnificent, almost a textbook on the use of plants: combining their shapes, textures and colours into a very satisfying picture. It is well worth taking time to pause here.

The basic colour is green as the foliage plays the major role, but it is lightened with touches of orange from the ligularia and in spring from *Caltha palustris* and the colour from various primulas. Hostas are the predominant plants, both plain and variegated ones. Their rounded, pleated leaves make a wonderful contrast to so many other kinds of foliage and here there is a very good clump of a blue-leaved variety in front of a gunnera, which in turn is overtopped by the pinnate leaves of a sumach. On either side there are more variegated hostas and the long strap-like leaves of iris, hemerocallis and grasses. The gunnera's large leaves are echoed elsewhere by the slightly smaller ones of *Rheum palmatum* and *Rodgersia polyphylla*. Altogether this makes a very pleasing picture, especially as it is all fronted by a sheet of water. It is possible to sit on the bench and look at this scene for a long time in complete tranquillity.

At the other end of this small triangular garden, is a border of complete contrast. It is devoted entirely to plants with golden foliage. This can be a bit of a cliché, especially when mixed with white flowering plants, but here it works extremely well and it is worth pausing as you pass to consider why.

Leaving this peaceful garden you enter one full of the hurly-burly of herbaceous borders. This is the part of the garden where flower-

Greencroft House. An example of the wonderful care for detail in this garden.

power comes into its own. There are far too many plants to mention individually. Already the reader will have gathered that this garden is put together by people who have an eye for these things and as will be expected the arrangement in this part of the garden is exquisite.

Most of the borders are dominated by one or more colours. Thus there is a hot border in which oranges, yellows and the hot reds dominate. At the opposite end of the garden is a border of blue and yellow. In between there is one of white and gold. Elsewhere there are combinations of purples and pinks. There is a great variety of plants in these borders without the overall appearance looking spotty, and visitors will doubtless be pleased to see that it is not only the rarer plants that can be used to good effect.

Moving on from here through the hedge, the visitor is startled by the starkness of the next garden, which is basically a lawn dominated on the far side by a 6 m (20 ft) holly hedge. The eye is drawn to the centre where there is a sundial on a plinth in the centre of a circular bed. This is planted with blue irises, surrounded by *Stachys byzantinum* and the carpeting *Acaena* 'Blue Haze' with its silver blue foliage. On the field side of the lawn there are some small semicircular beds, also planted with silver foliage plants. On the house side of the lawn there is an interesting double trellis covered with roses, clematis and honeysuckle.

The gaps through the tall hedge draw one like magnet. Through

63

the other side the visitors find themselves in a rectangular vegetable garden, divided by paths. Although vegetables are still grown here, quite a bit of the space is taken up with the cultivation of flowers that will be subsequently dried.

Passing through a new trellis and a hedge of rugosa roses, one again comes to a surprise: an area covered with gravel much in the style of a Japanese garden. However this is not an imitation of a Japanese garden, but a solution to a problem. It is an area where the washing is dried and where the grandchildren play. Until its transformation it tended to get a bit muddy and unkempt. With a polythene liner and a covering of stone chippings, it was given a dry and tidy surface. This has been enhanced by moving in some large rounded boulders and planting groups of grasses, conifers and a few shrubs. Sections of logs have also been arranged for children to sit and play on. The completed project is a very satisfying solution to what was a problem area. Washing can still be dried here and children can still play, but it is also a very attractive area to be in, again the shapes blending well with each other.

Leaving this area by way of a greenhouse, where most of the propagation is done, the visitor comes to a small triangular terrace hedged with roses (*Rosa* 'Maiden's Blush') underplanted with *Geranium macrorrhizum* and lily-of-the-valley *Convallaria majalis*. On the other side of the greenhouse, as a continuation of the trellis seen from the back lawn with the sundial, there is a pergola, made from the same rustic poles and covered with laburnum. This makes a pleasant, shady place to sit and relax out of the sun.

The visitor is now back on the paving in front of the house with its many pots and troughs. Immediately by the front door is a very fine plant of *Euphorbia rigida*, one of the best you are likely ever to see and providing a fitting climax to this magnificent garden.

The praise for this garden has been lavish, but then it deserves it. It cannot be more strongly recommended that this is a garden to visit. It often happens that a visitor will look at a garden such as this and say 'If only I had a garden like this I too could create something really worthwhile', but it must be remembered that all gardens start somewhere and that this was a wilderness when the owners started. They were not presented with the perfect garden in which to continue; they had to create it. Without intending to diminish the achievements of this garden in the slightest, it should be pointed out that such a garden should be within the capabilities of anyone. Visiting such a garden should not only provide the ideas, but also the stimulus for others to create their own perfect garden, not in imitation, but in their own right.

13
HALECAT

Witherslack

(Owned by Mrs Michael Stanley)

Aفتر driving through winding country lanes, you will find your pulse quickening in anticipation as you approach the gardens and nursery down a long curved drive. Having parked the car, you will be in a dilemma whether to go to the nursery or the gardens first. If there is any theory for the situation it would doubtless state that one should admire before purchasing, but most gardeners have an insatiable appetite for buying plants and perhaps the best policy is to go to the nursery and make your purchases and then proceed to the garden where, doubtless, desirable plants will be seen that will send you scurrying back to the nursery for a second visit.

Halecat is one of the main traditional nurseries of the Lakes. It has a wonderful old-fashioned air that applies not only to its somewhat ramshackle appearance but to the friendly and welcoming atmosphere imparted by the helpful staff. I shall give more detail in the chapter on nurseries, but it should be mentioned that the nursery here mainly concentrates on herbaceous plants, with a particularly good selection of hostas, with a few shrubs including one of the best collections of hydrangeas that you will find anywhere.

After an uncharacteristically quick visit to the nursery it is time for the visitor to move on to the garden. As is often the case with gardens attached to nurseries, it is free to enter, although the owners do make a charge for charities on a couple of days during the year.

The house was built in the mid-nineteenth century and the main garden lay-out was planned at about the same time. The present owners have lived and gardened here for more than forty years and so the planting as well as the structure of the garden has an established feeling about it. It basically consists of a stone terrace in

Open: *most of the year Mon–Fri, 9–4.30; Sun, 2–4; or by prior arrangement. Free except on charity opening days (see Yellow Book).*

Directions: *16 km (10 miles) sw of Kendal, on the edge of village of Witherslack. Nursery is signposted from A590.*

Access: *mostly level, with short flights of steps to lower gardens.*

Main attractions: *interesting terrace and herbaceous borders, nursery.*

Teas: *only on charity days.*

Plants for sale: *from nursery (see p. 153 for further details).*

Nearby gardens: *Holm Crag (17), Sizergh Castle (27), Levens Hall (19).*

front of the house that drops away to a lawn. Beyond this is a lower garden that leads to a summerhouse in one corner. From this and at the same level another garden extends back towards the side of the house. From the terrace, and also from the low lawn there are good views towards Arnside Knott. It is not a large garden, but then gardens do not have to be large to be interesting.

The garden has, surprisingly for the Lake District, an alkaline soil, due to the underlying limestone. In certain parts of the garden this stone has been excavated and used for walling, the resulting holes being refilled with an acid mixture which has allowed the growing of ericaceous plants such as rhododendrons and pieris.

It is always tempting to rush into a garden to get at the 'meat' of it, ignoring the plants on the way in, but do make time to pause along the side of the house and look at the plants there. In particular look at the *Leptospermum scoparium* 'Silver Sheen', with, as its name implies, incredible silvery foliage. This is a somewhat tender plant, but still well worth trying in a warm position, such as against a wall as here.

Once round to the back of the house, the visitor emerges onto the broad terrace that runs across the width of the house and has attractive views, as already mentioned. Do not be too distracted with the views as there are some interesting plantings here as well.

Halecat. Subtle colour combinations are one of the beauties of this garden. In this planting the pink of the roses combines perfectly with the purplish-green of the vine.

Halecat. There are several examples of the silvery foliage of *Rosa glauca* being used to perfection. Here it brilliantly sets off a daylily.

The shrubs on either side of the french doors are well chosen. There are balancing pairs, on one either side, of *Philadelphus microphyllus*, a *Ceanothus* and, peeping from behind with its straggly branches and beautiful white flowers, *Exochorda* × *macrantha* 'The Bride'. Another attraction is the plantings between the stones of the paving. In some cases the plants are potentially quite large such as the *Euphorbia myrsinites* while others are low carpeters like the *Acaena adscendens* (previously *A. affinis*). Ideal as the acaena are for planting on terraces, they are not for those gardeners who like to roam around barefooted, as they have rather prickly burs. Another small plant used successfully here is *Alchemilla conjuncta*, which has darkish green leaves edged with silver that is also found on the reverse. A final feature of this terrace are the black and white tubs of *Lilium regale* that adorn it during the summer.

Immediately in front of the terrace a steep bank leads down to a large expanse of lawn. To the left of the lawn, on the same level as the terrace, a broad path leads to the steps above the lower garden. To the left of this path is the main herbaceous border. Although it is convenient to describe it thus, it is not strictly an herbaceous border as it also contains a number of shrubs including roses. Although there are plants in flower at other times of year, it is during the summer that this border is at its best with geraniums, veronica, phloxes, echinops, euphorbias and many more herbaceous plants. One normally thinks of clematis as being woody perennials, but there are a few herbaceous forms that die back each year. In this border is *Clematis recta*, which is best in its form 'Purpurea'. This cultivar produces beautiful purple foliage when it first starts to appear in spring; later it reverts to green although still slightly tinged with purple. The flowers are small, but their massed effect, followed by their seed heads, gives a long season of interest. It is a very floppy plant and does need support to be effective.

At the end of the path are two obelisks, marking the top of the steps leading to the lower garden. Although attractive in their own right both are obscured by even more attractive plantings. A purple vine scrambles over one, around the base of which, and through which twines *Rosa* 'Raubritter'; the pink and purple making an effective combination.

There are some very interesting combinations in the lower garden. In early spring the effect of the yellow *Paeonia mlokosewitschii* underplanted with pink *Dicentra formosana* is a bit startling, but later in the season there are some very nice juxtapositions. One of the most imaginative is the use of *Crambe cordifolia*. There are several plants of this, both in this garden and in the one that stretches back to the house, each used in ways that are extremely effective. Normally this plant is given plenty of space so that its enormous froth of flowers can be appreciated as a specimen plant; here it is planted tightly with other plants so that it grows through them. In the lower garden it erupts through *Rosa glauca* (*R. rubrifolia*). This is particularly effective in the latter flowering stages when only a few isolated flowers float in an ethereal way amongst the rose's branches. Another nice combination with a *Rosa glauca* is an underplanting of the silver-leaved *Anaphalis triplinervis* with the upright stems of the white-flowered *Verbascum chaixii* 'Album' and flowers of a near-by *Rosa* 'Iceberg' peeping through the silver foliage. The purple centres of the verbascum flowers are echoed in the nearby *Geranium psilostemon*.

Yet another association with the *Rosa glauca* (surely an underrated plant) is the rather unexpected appearance of a reddish mahogany hemerocallis through and amongst the glaucous pinkish foliage of the rose. This may not sound very beautiful, but the effect is stunning and well worth emulating. A final combination in the adjacent garden is to grow blue delphiniums amongst the silver leaves of several rose bushes.

Having moved into the garden that goes back to the house, you should take a backward glance at the very attractive summerhouse with its gothic windows and the paved area around it. This makes a good contrast to the rest of the garden and creates an intimate corner with far-reaching views.

Originally the last garden must have been a long thin narrow space but it has now been broken by a series of iron trellises that form baffles along its length. These are treated in different ways, one of which is the planting of pink roses (*R.* 'Fantin Latour') under *Cotinus coggygria* 'Royal Purple' capped with a bluish purple clematis, possibly *Clematis jackmanii* which has an overlap with the rose, and adds colour to the cotinus later in the season.

These trellises work very effectively as visual barriers and also create a series of small gardens, each with its own character. There is a lot of white in this area. *Crambe cordifolia* again occurs in several combinations. One very effective one consists of two plants placed behind an urn, the rounded shapes of the crambe seeming to form hazy handles on each side of the container. Again this is particularly effective once the main flowering is over and there are just a few small white flowers delicately held by the thin airy branches. There is much to explore in this part of the garden.

Finally you will arrive back at the lawn and the plantings on its two lower sides. These are possibly the least successful in the garden, at least in the summer when the backing of philadelphus and the underplanting of various geraniums are both over. There are bushes of potentilla to add some colour, but these are pale and when planted en masse can be a bit boring. Stronger colours could possibly be used here to advantage.

This then is a very interesting garden with many good colour combinations, many involving purple, pink and white. Philadelphus are obviously popular plants here and an early summer visit when these are in flower will add considerably to the pleasure. Like most gardens, the combinations of the plants in flower are always changing and frequent visitors to the nursery should always make a point of popping through the gate just to see what is happening.

Halecat. A beautiful summerhouse nestles amongst the trees at the bottom of the garden with views towards the coast.

14
HILL TOP

The village of Near Sawrey, near Hawkshead

(Owned by the National Trust)

Open: *April–Oct, 11–5. Closed Thurs, Fri. £3.20 for house and garden (no garden-only tickets). Free to NT members.*

Directions: *3 km (2 miles) s of Hawkshead, at Near Sawrey. Small car park.*

Access: *level, but with narrow paths. Walk from car park is 183 m (200 yd) along narrow, busy road.*

Main attractions: *traditional cottage garden, incorporating vegetables and fruit; Beatrix Potter connection.*

Teas: *village teashops and NT-owned pub.*

Plants for sale: *no*

Nearby gardens: *Graythwaite (11). Grizedale Forest also nearby.*

VERY FEW people intentionally visit this garden, but thousands pass through it every year on their way to the cottage in which Beatrix Potter lived. It was here that she wrote many of her Peter Rabbit books. The garden is not particularly outstanding, although it is a good example of what is considered to be an old-fashioned cottage garden — a style of gardening that many read about, but rarely see in reality.

The public enter through the National Trust shop next to the road and walk the length of the garden to get to the house. In doing so they pass through a mixture of vegetables, fruit and flowers, which although allotted their own space, tend to merge, making one satisfying picture. The shape is typical of many old cottage gardens, long and narrow, with an area of flowers near the house. There is a clear space outside the door, but no real lawn. Very few cottage gardens bothered with lawns, there was no time to lounge around and, besides, there was the necessity of cutting them by hand. If any sitting around was indulged in, perhaps while carrying out some chores such as mending or preparing vegetables, or possibly just gossiping, it was more likely to be carried out on a bench near the front door. It is not surprising to find that just such a bench exists at Hill Top.

Vegetables and fruit were a vital part of a cottage economy and both ground and time were given over to them. Here at Hill Top there are two areas devoted to their cultivation. One is towards the bottom of the long garden, near the shop, and the other is in a small enclosed garden immediately in front of the cottage. While both played such an important role in the past, vegetable growing seems to be on the decline in the Lake District with very few of the gardens, compared to other parts of the country, showing

signs of them. It is a pleasure, therefore to see them at Hill Top.

Since medieval times fruit has played an equal, if not at times a more important role, than vegetables, in many gardens where it would often be used for making drinks of various sorts as well as for use as food. For the cottagers it was possibly the only form of food that did not taste bland. Nowadays with fruit so readily available from all over the world, either fresh from greengrocers or preserved in tins or jars, it is difficult to remember that in the past the main way of acquiring it was to grow it yourself. A lot of fruit is still grown at Hill Top; the garden behind the house being mainly devoted to strawberries, raspberries, currants, gooseberries and rhubarb. However, there is an old orchard just over the fence and a

Hill Top. A reconstruction of a typical Lakeland cottage garden provides a colourful approach to Beatrix Potter's house.

71

Hill Top. Beatrix Potter's home is everybody's romantic image of a cottage with scented roses surrounding the door and windows.

few other fruit trees, including a cherry, growing in the garden.

Most of the garden, however, is given over to flowers and here both the style of planting and the plants themselves reflect the cottage garden that it is. The flowers are mainly old-fashioned ones, many, such as the honeysuckle (*Lonicera periclymenum*), foxgloves (*Digitalis purpurea*) and the sweet cicely (*Myrrhis odorata*), derived from native plants that can be seen in the hedgerows. There are many old favourites here such as lupins, single peonies, lavender and philadelphus. Cottage gardens were not all simple flowers; surprisingly exotic plants such as lilies have been grown in them for a long time, seed and bulbils probably finding their way out of the bigger gardens in gardeners' pockets, or old bulbs were perhaps rescued from bygone compost heaps of the well-to-do. One of the lilies commonly seen was *Lilium pyrenaicum* with its yellow turk's-cap flowers and this can be seen here at Hill Top in the early summer. Its foxy odour can also be smelt, even if you don't have a very sensitive nose, and many people find it objectionable.

As well as flowering plants for their decorative quality there are also many that would have been grown for their medicinal or culinary qualities; amongst others, feverfew (*Tanecetum parthenium*) useful for headaches, and angelica (*Angelica archangelica*) for the kitchen are both to be found in these colourful borders. The low-growing sweet woodruff, *Galium odorata*, with its tiny white starry flowers also grows here. This would have been used for its sweet smell, possibly strewn on the floor or placed in the linen or into mattresses. Lavender would also have been used to ward off everyday odours.

All these plants are planted in an almost haphazard way with all the colours and shapes mingled in a way that only seems to work in a cottage garden. Plants are put in where there are gaps, with scant regard for their neighbours and self-sowers dot themselves all over the place. In the Lake District, the Welsh poppy, *Meconopsis cambrica*, is the doyen of self-sowers and is likely to crop up unexpectedly even in formal gardens. Here also there is also the red valerian, *Centranthus ruber*, which loves to grow in old walls, as well as columbines, *Aquilegia vulgaris*, and mulleins, *Verbascum*, springing up here and there to add to the pattern of colour and form.

Cottages are typically depicted with roses round the door and Hill Top is no exception. It also has two other characteristic cottage plants clambering over it. Japonica, as *Chaenomeles* is confusingly known, is certainly an old favourite as is wisteria. The wall dividing the garden from other properties is also clothed with climbers, including more wisteria, roses and a vine.

Hill Top is not amongst the top rank of gardens in the Lake District, but none the less it is interesting to visit a cottage garden that cannot have changed much since the nineteenth century.

15
HOLEHIRD
Near Windermere

(Owned by Lakeland Horticultural Society)

Open: *all year, 9–dusk. Free but donations welcomed.*

Directions: *Just NE of Windermere. Take A592 towards Patterdale and Ullswater and Holehird is less than 1.5 km (1 mile) on R.*

Access: *Mostly gentle slopes, except rock garden.*

Main attractions: *walled garden with summer borders and herb bed, alpine house, rock garden, winter garden. Most plants labelled. National collection of shield ferns, astilbes and hydrangeas.*

Teas: *picnic area beside tarn. Teashops in Windermere.*

Plants for sale: *nearest nurseries at Halecat (13) and Hayes near Ambleside, but on 1st Sat in May, LHS holds very popular, good value plant sale at Lakeside School (expect queues).*

Nearby gardens: *Stagshaw (28).*

DEMONSTRATION gardens are not always as good as they should be and often end up showing what should not be done rather than what should be. Holehird is in the capable hands of the enthusiasts of the Lakeland Horticultural Society and sets a positive standard that is well worth emulating.

The gardens are set within the grounds of the Holehird Estate which is administered by Cumbria County Council. The Society leases nearly five acres for its gardens. The house is leased separately to the Leonard Cheshire Foundation as a nursing home. The house and the paths adjacent to it are not open to the public, but the gardens that lie in front, although not part of the LHS gardens, are open to visitors.

The Lakeland Horticultural Society was set up in 1969 and two years later leased the major part of its present grounds. In 1978 it managed to spread its wings a bit further to obtain the walled garden, then the remains of a forestry nursery previously a kitchen garden. Although overgrown through lack of attention during the World War II the basic framework of the garden in the form of the rock garden and some of the mature trees was already in place.

The garden consists of several quite distinct areas. Nearest to the car park is the walled garden. This was taken over by the LHS in 1978, but it was not until three years later that they were in a position to start planting. Once the old glasshouses had been cleared from the site the members were confronted with a completely empty space. The central area was put down to grass and borders in front of two walls were dug to provide homes for herbaceous plants. A third border was used as a nursery bed with a few cold frames in one corner. On the fourth side of the square was built a members' room where glass sides look across a paved area to the borders. In the corner of this paved area a small herb garden was created. All have now matured, as have a couple of borders placed diagonally across the centre of the lawn.

The plants in these borders are all labelled. Often similar plants are placed near each other so that the difference can be seen. Thus *Brunnera macrophylla* is next to its two variegated forms *B.m.* 'Variegata' and *B.m.* 'Hadspen Cream'. It doesn't always quite work out like this. Hours can be spent trekking the thirty yards between plants labelled as *Stachys grandiflora* in one border and those as *S. macrantha* in the other, trying to work out what the subtle difference is between them only to discover later that they are in fact the same plant and that the correct name is now the latter!

These borders are undoubtedly at their best in the summer months with a wide variety of herbaceous plants then in flower, including various *Dactylorhiza* orchids, but there are also things to see earlier in the season, including some rhododendrons in the central beds. Being labelled, albeit occasionally with the name being a little out of date, certainly adds to the interest and usefulness of this garden.

Moving through the gate of this garden and passing the Society's offices the visitor comes to the alpine house. This is a delightfully old-fashioned structure, but none the less extremely functional. As with many of the older alpine houses it is set into the ground, in this case into the slope of the hill. This means that the house stays relatively warm during cold spells, partly because the soil below the benches acts as a large storage heater and partly because being lower it is less prone to wind chill. Many such glasshouses can bring tender plants through a winter without the need of extra heat and it is still a method of construction that commends itself if one has more ability than is normally required simply to put up a modern kit glasshouse. These comments apply to all forms of glasshouse not just alpine houses, although the latter generally do not require to be kept warm, their main function being to keep out the rain and possibly cold desiccating winds. This alpine house is furnished with tufa cliffs in which a wide range of plants happily exist with their roots going deep down into the rock.

Just outside the alpine house is a fine plant of *Crinodendron hookerianum* with its large red lanterns set off against the dark evergreen leaves. At its feet in early summer a very fine clump of bright blue *Gentiana acaulis* may be seen, not an easy plant to grow successfully.

Moving up the hill the visitor comes to the rock garden. On the lower side of this the rock is clearly exposed and the plantings are of typical alpine plants. Some of these have been here many years and have established large clumps, others, as is their wont, have wandered about, often appearing long distances from where they were planted, leaving their labels in splendid isolation. Looking at labels in rock gardens must always be done with care. They do not always apply to the nearest plant, sometimes they may have wandered as just mentioned, but at other times the plant that the label refers to may have retired below ground for the summer, leaving nothing to be seen, and causing the unwary to erroneously attribute the name to another nearby plant. There are of course numerous occasions when the plant has simply died and the label has been unintentionally left in the ground as some sort of inadvertent memorial.

In the upper half of the rock garden, the rock is largely covered with trees and shrubs, many of them unusual. There are some particularly fine monkey puzzle trees, *Araucaria auracana*, with trunks that are covered with branches right to the ground. Amongst other woody plants are several acers, conifers, including a large specimen of *Sciadopterys verticiliata*, camellias, and, of course, rhododendrons and azaleas. Berberis are becoming quite commonplace in gardens, but one of the most unusual species grown here is *B. valdiviana*, which has long tassels of yellow flowers, rather like pendant earrings, well set off against the large glossy green leaves.

There are also odd pockets of interesting herbaceous plants. Near the top, for example, there is a little grove of meconopsis in which quite a number of species are represented. Another interesting collection, up in the top corner, is that of ferns, of which Holehird contains the national collection of the shield ferns, *Polystichum*. Again everything is labelled making it a useful garden to visit if you wish to identify plants.

On the north side of this garden there are heather borders and further north still in the apex of the garden is the winter garden which is filled with plants that flower during this time of year, before spring gets under way. These include the winter heathers, *Daphne mezereum*, hellebores, witch hazel (*Hamamelis*), snowdrops, (*Galanthus*) and the early flowering rhododendron, *R. praecox*.

Following round from the winter gardens, the beds that are on the lower side of the lawns, below the drive, contain the main plantings of roses. These have been enterprisingly underplanted with a number of different geraniums. Further round these borders is Holehird's national collection of astilbes, rather a brash sight when they are all in flower. Continuing round the corner of this long border the visitor comes to the main part of another national

Holehird. One is always aware of the plants in this garden framing the Lakeland landscape.

collection, the hydrangeas. These are seen at their best in flower towards the end of the summer.

Between this lower border and the rock areas above is the main grass area which during the spring is full of narcissi as well as other bulbs such as *Erythronium dens-canis* and *Fritillaria meleagris*. These two plus *Anemone blanda*, lesser celandines and dandelions, make a delightful spring display on the little knoll where several paths meet just outside the car park — a wonderful piece of natural planting.

Connecting the hydrangea beds and the rock garden is a long shady border in which many woodland plants are grown. There are some good clumps of *Rodgersia* here as well as a wonderful display of hostas. Although the latter only represent a fraction of the many thousands that are now in existence, they make a useful reference collection for those struggling to differentiate between them. Of all the herbaceous plants, grasses and ferns excluded, they must be one of the most confusing groups, with often only minor differences between them. Providing a lot of the shade of this

Holehird. One of the earliest parts of this garden to be constructed was the magnificent rock gardens, which display a wide range of alpines.

border is one of the most magnificent sights in the whole garden — a huge *Davidia involucrata*. For those who do not know this tree a visit in June is a must as then it is covered with small, almost insignificant flowers that look like black buttons, surrounded by huge white bracts that hang like pieces of cloth, hence its vernacular name, handkerchief tree. It is particularly splendid in a year following a hot summer when a lot of flower buds will have formed. Any gardener who beholds this tree when it is in full flower and does not find his breath taken away has not got a soul.

Apart from a few interesting climbers on the wall of the car park this is the full extent of the Lakeland Horticultural Society's garden. However the gardens in front of the house, which are administered by the County Council, are also open to the public. This starts with the delightful planting round the pools just opposite the entrance to the car park. A stroll round the paths, avoiding the ones immediately around the house to provide those that live there some privacy, will reveal many joys in both the plantings and in the views. The latter are especially good from the fountain. To most visitors the fells are as difficult to name as hostas, but the LHS produces a guide to the garden which includes a drawing naming all that can be seen from this position. A short walk away is Holehird Tarn which makes a delightful place to picnic.

It was a wonderful idea for the LHS to set up its own gardens and it is to their credit that they have carried out their intentions so well. It is refreshing to be able to enter a garden of this type without having to run the gauntlet of high pressure sales in the form of a shop with all kinds of unwanted items that could equally have come from Cornwall as the Lake District. The Society is constantly present, in the form of volunteers housed in a discreet office (often to be seen sitting outside if it is sunny!) for those who want information. They are always very friendly and helpful, and one is left with the impression that they appreciate that the purpose of your visit is to see the garden and avoid all the tourist hype that often encumbers other national gardens. This does not mean that they are not interested in your money as, after all, they have an expensive garden to keep up, but they rely on voluntary contributions placed in the donation boxes in the car park or in the wall of the office. Do give generously.

Perhaps it is because of the fact that most of the plants are labelled that one sees so many visitors stopping and discussing each plant as they pass, or perhaps it is because they have so many interesting plants. Either way visitors always seem at ease at Holehird; there never seems to be any rush to get round and see everything in five minutes and get away. It is a pleasant garden to stroll around looking at and learning from all there is to see. As with so many gardens in the Lake District, one of the great joys of Holehird is the wonderful glimpses of water and distant fells. Lake Windermere can be seen from several places in the garden, and, although not overwhelming here, one is always aware of the beautiful surrounding hills.

16
HOLKER HALL
Cark-in-Cartmel

(Owned by Lord and Lady Cavendish)

Open: *Easter–end Oct, 10.30–6. Closed Sat. £2.75. House also open.*

Directions: *6.5 km (4 miles) W of Grange-over-Sands. Signposted from A590 on to B5278 through Haverthwaite, then on to B5277 via Grange and Cark. Ample parking.*

Access: *mostly easy, except for higher reaches.*

Main attractions: *formal garden and cascade, flower meadow, rose garden, unusual shrubs.*

Teas: *tearoom in stableyard.*

Plants for sale: *limited selection. Nearest nurseries T. H. Barker and Halecat.*

Nearby gardens: *Sizergh Castle (27), Levens Hall (19), Underfields (30), Halecat (13), Holm Crag (17).*

A VISIT TO THE gardens at Holker is part of a day out for the whole family as there are many other attractions to be enjoyed. They are probably the best known gardens in the Lake District with thousands of visitors enjoying the 8 hectares (20 acres) each year, especially in late spring when the rhododendrons are at their peak.

Holker Hall is the home of the Cavendish family who have tended the gardens since at least the 1720s. Towards the end of that century the formal gardens were replaced by a more natural type of landscape garden and to a certain extent this is still the idea behind a large part of the garden, which consists mainly of trees, shrubs and grass. In more recent times it has followed this philosophy to its modern conclusion by including a flower meadow within the garden. The gardens were again revised by Lady Moyra Cavendish who came to live at Holker Hall at the beginning of the twentieth century. Thomas Mawson, who also designed Graythwaite and Brockhole, came to the Hall and designed, among other things, the rose garden. Much of the plantings of trees and shrubs that we see today date from the time of Lady Moyra, who had a lasting influence on the garden.

However, time has not been allowed to ossify the garden. Recently two of the areas near to the house have been redesigned and planted. These are the first two gardens that the visitor sees on entering the gate by the house. The first is a Formal Garden with a geometric layout. The beds of this square garden have been created by making a wide circular path and then bisecting the resulting central bed with two further paths at right angles to each other.

The planting of these beds is a mixture of shrubs and herbaceous plants with a predominance of the latter. It is still young and, as with all newly planted borders, the colours and heights are not quite right so a certain amount of adjustment will be required. The principal colours are blues, whites, pinks and silver, but there is one border where pale yellows are admitted. The plants are all familiar (none the worse for that), including geraniums, hemerocallis, lilies, delphiniums, penstemons, peonies and so one, giving a long season of colour. It will be interesting to see how this garden develops over the years.

The public is not allowed into the main gardens behind the house, but there is a small area of bedding (echium, edged with *Alchemilla mollis*) near the house from which these gardens can be seen. The yew hedges here have the familiar Lakeland practice of having *Tropaeolum speciosum* growing through them.

The next garden, the Summer Garden, has been planted slightly longer and is showing signs of becoming established. This is a bit more elaborate in design and includes pleached Portuguese laurels, *Prunus lusitanicus*, which will eventually meet over the top of a metal pergola, turning the central path into a shady walkway. Although a summer garden, it is beautiful in spring with massed plantings of tulips and spring bedding plants, with flowering cherries. In the summer there is also plenty of bedding here to give colour throughout the summer. In the side borders there are also plantings of herbaceous plants and a few shrubs. There is a particularly good combination of *Macleaya cordata*, and *Eremurus* and a pinkish *Hemerocallis*.

At the far end of the Summer Garden is a rather fine gate leading into a flower meadow. Here the grass is allowed to grow until after mid summer so that a variety of wild flowers can blossom and seed. Paths have been mown through it so that visitors have a chance of wandering through the flowers. Late spring and early summer is the best time for this part of the garden.

The other exit from the Summer Garden, to the right of the gate into the flower meadow, leads one into the more informal part of the garden, in which, at least at the lower levels, rhododendrons predominate. Around these as the walk begins are several interesting plantings of primulas and meconopsis, the latter including the red-flowered *M. napaulensis*.

Further on the visitor comes to the cascade, a feature not seen frequently in British gardens. Unlike most other Lakeland gardens, which virtually all seem to have natural streams and waterfalls, here the water has been tamed and falls down either side of a wide flight of steps in two channels that curl away at the bottom. Also at the bottom is a round pool with a fountain playing in the centre. The steps are shaded by tall *Rhododendron arboreum*, which in the

Holker Hall. A subtle combination of colours in the Summer Garden provided by macleaya, eremurus and hemerocallis.

spring carpet the ground with their cerise petals, and other trees, including the stately holm oak, *Quercus ilex*, and the beautiful fern-leaved or cut-leaved beech, *Fagus sylvatica* 'Aspleniifolia' (formerly *F.s. heterophylla*). At the top, dominating the steps in the bright sunlight, is an imposing statue of Neptune casting his eyes away to the Rose Garden beyond. The cascade was built between 1988 and 1991, but the fountain has been in existence for 150 years.

The Rose Garden can either be approached direct, across the lawns from Neptune, or along the paths to the right. From the latter springs a long pergola, designed, along with the Rose Garden itself, by Thomas Mawson around the beginning of this century. The curved pergola approaches the garden under swags of climbing roses and clematis, as well as the more unusual climber *Schisandra rubriflora* (now considered a separate species from *S. grandiflora*). The pergola also has other plants, such as *Lilium regale* and geraniums planted along its base. The delightful rose garden is semicircular, with a summerhouse (now inhabited by white doves), in one corner and an arbour and pool in the other. Two light and airy gazebos, with roses and honeysuckle growing over them are placed on the curved side of the garden.

As well as roses there are a few underplantings, some of which rather jar with the predominantly pink roses. For example, in one bed there is *Euphorbia griffithii* whose flame-orange bracts somewhat clash with the pink tulips in spring and in summer with the pink flowers of *R*. 'Quatre Saisons' on one side and the purple of *R*. 'Tour de Malakoff' on the other. Similarly in the opposite bed the pink and purple are backed with the yellow flowers of fennel, the lime green of *Nicotiania langdorfii* and the acid yellow of *Jasminum humile* — not a comfortable association of colours.

The rhododendrons in this garden are generally set in parkland

Holker Hall (*opposite*). One of the attractions of this garden is a long flight of steps flanked by cascading water. In spring the rhododendron petals carpet the ground.

83

conditions, often surrounded by large areas of lawns, so that when in flower they appear to be billowing clouds. This makes a useful contrast to other gardens, such as Stagshaw, where they are densely planted amongst other shrubs and trees on steep hillsides, that give an impression of the rhododendron's homeland of the Himalayan mountains.

Probably the most absorbing part of the garden is higher up the slopes, towards the Haverthwaite Road, where a large number of interesting trees and shrubs have been planted. Many, such as *Carpenteria californica* or the nearby *Hoheria lyallii*, are marginally tender and yet manage to survive at the top of the slope, up against the wall of the garden. Holker Hall is not far from the coast and benefits from the relatively warm influence of the Gulf Stream. For anyone interested in trees and shrubs this is a wonderful area to wander through, with a welter of less familiar plants to look at. There are a number of different magnolias, viburnums and cornus that can be enjoyed when in flower.

It is worth the effort to come here in the autumn to see the colouring of such plants as *Oxydendron arboreum*, *Lindera obtusiloba*, *Stewartia ovata* and *S. pseudocamellia koreana*. These plus many others are, of course, also very interesting while in flower. Amongst these is *Decaisnea fargesii*, which is becoming increasingly popular with its untidy lime green flowers and spectacular blue seed pods. Another plant with intriguing seed pods is *Staphylea holocarpa*. This has deutzia-type pink flowers, followed this time by inflated pods, like blown-up paper bags. *Caragana arborescens* is a shrub with yellow pea-like flowers. It has three main cultivars of which 'Lorbergii' is represented here. *Halesia* is another genus worthy of mention. Both *H. carolina* and *H. monticola* have dainty white bells (hence the vernacular name of Carolina silverbell), the latter being larger in all its parts, forming a small tree rather than a shrub.

There are a few climbers of note in this upper part of the garden. There is a particularly spectacular plant of *Rosa* 'Cedric Morris' which rambles 6 m (20 ft) or more up into an oak tree. The white flowers are set off beautifully against the greyish-green leaves around mid summer.

An extremely informative, illustrated guide to the woodland garden can be bought from the shop and should be purchased *before* going in as it gives two walks around this part of the garden, naming the trees and shrubs, as you progress.

Holker Hall has large gardens, which can be enjoyed at any time of the year. Taken in association with the other attractions it can provide a whole day's entertainment.

17
HOLM CRAG
Near Witherslack

(Owned by Jack Watson)

MOST OF THE better gardens that are open to the public in a particular area are usually documented in some form or another. Just occasionally one comes across a garden with an 'open' sign on the gate that is not listed anywhere. There is often a slight reluctance to enter as what lies beyond the gate is unknown, and being candid, can be embarrassing to the visitor. This is one such unheard-of garden, which is tucked away in the narrow lanes behind Witherslack, that should be entered with no hesitation.

It is an unusual garden in many respects, none more so than that the gardener, Jack Watson, is a retired farmer. Farmers don't generally like gardening (naturally enough perhaps), although some are reluctantly dragooned by their wives to do the heavy work. When Jack and his wife retired to Holm Crag, it was his wife who started the garden. Jack became interested and started to help and when his wife died the garden became almost his full-time occupation.

The next unusual thing about this garden is that it is a very natural garden, nothing seems forced in it and yet it is obviously under Jack's control. To one side the ground rises steeply with a magnificent natural rock garden, on the other is natural woodland and down the middle a lawn leading to a large pond and a boggy area with natural vegetation taking over beyond this. Many people take a garden and try unsuccessfully to convert it into a wild garden, ending up with a lot of unruly weeds. Jack has taken a piece of wild land and sympathetically tamed some of it leaving the rest to its own devices, blending together the two elements in a way that few other gardeners have managed. A third interesting thing about this garden arises out of the last. Jack is extremely interested in wildlife and is never more happy than when birds, mammals and

Open: *nearly all the time. Donation to Cumbrian Wildlife Trust.*

Directions: *near Witherslack. From A590 follow signs to Halecat (see 13). Holm Crag is about 1 km (⅔ mile) beyond Halecat nursery on L, past small bridge. Roadside parking.*

Access: *much of garden visible from drive and lawn, but rock garden and beyond require agility.*

Main attractions: *wildlife garden, with pond and bog garden, large rock garden, veranda of tender plants.*

Teas: *nearby villages worth exploring for teashops; Old Vicarage Country House Hotel, Witherslack.*

Plants for sale: *seasonal cut flowers; Halecat Nursery close by.*

Nearby gardens: *Halecat (13), Levens Hall (19), Sizergh Castle (27)*

insects visit his garden. The natural setting obviously helps. The variety of terrain and trees and bushes means that there are plenty of differing nest sites, so much so that one year there were an incredible 32 different species nesting within the garden. It is not at all surprising that Jack has won awards for the best bird garden in 1989 and also for his efforts in raising money for the Cumbrian Wildlife Trust.

The approach to the garden down the drive is rather sombre under tall conifers, but it is soon brightened by many bright red and pink flowering succulents hanging from the porch and in the hollowed out logs along the front of the bungalow. They glow through the shade. One is also immediately aware of the rock climbing away to the right of the drive. This has been uncovered and makes one of the best natural rock gardens that one can see anywhere. Its scale is large enough to allow Jack to include plants such as the border penstemons and hemerocallis as well as the more delicate alpines. This use of bigger plants means that there is plenty of colour later in the season as well as in the spring when the alpines are at their height. Above the rock are shrubs and smaller trees, including many that produce berries for the birds and other animals. Jack will take you by a path from near the entrance of the drive which leads way up above the rock garden. Here many wild plants, including foxgloves (*Digitalis purpurea*) and viper's bugloss (*Echium vulgare*), are allowed to seed around. Some cultivated plants, such as michaelmas daisies (*Aster novi-belgii*) have also been introduced for their autumn seed heads.

In front of the bungalow is a lawn which stretches parallel with the rock garden down to the pond. On its left is another, much lower outcrop of rock. This includes some interesting and attractive alpines including pulsatilla (which have to be caged against the rabbits) and the wonderful silver-leaved *Hieracum lanatum*. Part of this outcrop is planted with heathers.

The planting beside the pond is magnificent and could never be thought of as dull as its main ingredient is a large swathe of bright astilbes above which are hemerocallis in variety. There is a small feeder pool surrounded by rocks over which scambles a number of different thymes. It is very unusual to see water rimmed by what is usually considered to be a plant for dry places (the surrounding rocks are of course very free-draining), but it is a very successful planting. On this outcrop is a wonderful planting of *Dicentra formosana* and a large clump of *Codonopsis*. Also in this area, up amongst the rocks above the pond is a large patch of dark sidalcea.

Below the pond the garden returns to the wild with great swathes of meadowsweet (*Filipendula ulmaria*) colouring it cream in the summer. This is in the low-lying area through which the pond ultimately drains. Before entering this, however, any excess water passes through a more cultivated damp patch on the left of the pond. Here the flowers are predominantly yellow with drifts of yellow loosestrife (*Lysimachia punctata*), plume poppy (*Macleaya cordata*), various inulas, *Cephalaria gigantea*, the giant rhubarb (*Rheum palmatum*), and the bright magenta *Lychnis chalcedonica*.

Beyond some shrubs is the vegetable garden where Jack grows all that he requires to keep the kitchen supplied. Past this is a path into the woods at the side of the house. Down here are a variety of meconopsis including the not frequently seen yellow species *M. chelidoniifolia*. There is also a patch of *Uvularia grandiflora*, a plant one would expect to see more frequently in this area. It is a woodlander with its petals hanging like small pieces of twisted yellow rag. Jack is not immune (and nor should he be) from the Lakeland habit of growing *Tropaeolum speciosum* up through conifers, the flame red of the flowers making a wonderful contrast with the dark green of the trees.

Back at the bungalow it is worth looking at the colourful display

Holm Crag. Astibles, hemerocallis, loosestrife and other brightly coloured plants clothe the slopes above the pond.

of plants in pots on the veranda. These are usually taken inside during the winter so that plants, such as the purple climber *Rhodochiton atrosanguineus*, are able to grow to a large size. One of the most spectacular plants here is one that will also grow in the open border, *Michauxia campanuloides*. Its large exotic white flowers are more reminiscent of passion flowers than of the campanulas to which it belongs. There are several bulbs here including, in mid summer, a superb pot of deep red amaryllis, *Hippeastrum*. This veranda is a garden in its own right and it would be well worth coming to Holm Crag just to see it alone if there were not so much else to see and appreciate.

Any gardeners in the area should visit this garden. If you are interested in encouraging wildlife then it is even more important that you should not miss it. Jack Watson is usually to be found somewhere around the garden and makes an informative, self-effacing guide for a quick tour before fading into the background to let you look around on your own. The tamed naturalness of this garden will undoubtedly make it the favourite of many Lakeland visitors and residents alike.

Holm Crag. A natural rock garden has been created by exposing the underlying stone on the slopes that dominate this garden.

18
HUTTON-IN-THE-FOREST

Near Penrith

(Owned by Lord and Lady Inglewood)

THIS GARDEN is currently going through one of its many transformations over the centuries. In recent times it has been but a sad reflection of times past, but now, due to the keenness of its owners and the ability of its gardener, Hutton-in-the-Forest is again becoming somewhere that is well worth visiting. As yet the transformation has only occurred near to the house, but one hopes that it will continue into the surrounding woods which have been sadly neglected.

The first indication of this is the sudden revelation of a garden on the east end of the southern terraces. After walking along broad gravel paths from the car park you enter a small, curved sloping garden dominated by an old water pump. This is full of colour especially in spring when it is vivid with the red, white, pink, yellow and orange of various candelabra primulas such as *P. japonica*, *P. pulverulenta* and *P. chungensis*. These hotter colours are set off against the cooler blues of forget-me-nots (*Myosotis*), the coarse *Pentaglottis sempervirens* and *Brunnera macrophylla*, the last including the variegated form as well as the ordinary species. There are also some attractive clumps of *Persicara bistorta* (*Polygonatum bistortum*) whose columns of pink flowers always look so fresh against the green leaves. Other spring flowers include *Pulmonaria rubra* and *P. saccharata*, and *Daphne mezereum*. Later comes the yellow tree peony *Paeonia lutea ludlowii* and the blue poppies, *Meconopis betonicifolia* and *M. grandis*. The pendent tubular flowers of *Polygonatum* × *hybridum*, Solomon's seal, also appear at this time of year.

Structure is given to this garden by various shrubs including the ubiquitous rhododendron and ground cover is provided by *Tiarella cordifolia* as well as some of the plants already mentioned. At the back of the bed on the east side of the path is a rather nice planting

Open: *most of the year, 11–5. Closed Sat. £1. House open end May–end June, Thurs, Fri, Sun, Bank Hol. Mon, 1–4. £1 (£2.80 to include house).*

Directions: *near village of Unthank, on B5305, 5 km (3 miles) NW of Junction 41 of M6. Ample parking.*

Access: *mostly flat; remoter parts may be boggy in wet weather.*

Main attractions: *spring 'pump' garden, woodland, wild-flower meadow. Much still being restored.*

Teas: *tearoom in house.*

Plants for sale: *no*

Nearby gardens: *Dalemain (7).*

of the bright blue comfrey, *Symphytum asperulum*, next to great mounds of the yellow greater celandine, *Chelidonium majus*.

From the joy and gaiety of this little corner one moves along the front of the house, along the south terraces. The area immediately in front is left to rough grass with wild flowers allowed to grow in it. The attractive planting includes water avens (*Geum rivale*), pignut (*Conopodium majus*), cow parsley (*Anthriscus sylvestris*), self-heal (*Prunella vulgaris*), crosswort (*Galium cruciata*), cowslips (*Primula veris*), dandelions (*Taraxacum officinale*), buttercups (*Ranunculus*), milkmaids or cuckoo-flower (*Cardamine pratensis*) in the damper parts, germander speedwell (*Veronica chamaedrys*), and a large clump of the later-flowering pheasant's eye narcissus (*N. poeticus*).

Below this wild flower meadow is what was a large area of rhododendron and yews, criss-crossed with paths which ultimately lead down to one of the lakes. This has become very overgrown with many of the rhododendron reverting to their rather boring rootstock of *R. ponticum*. This area was originally laid out in 1870 by Lady Vane as a rhododendron garden, and although the inter-locking paths have been opened up again the planting needs a great

Hutton-in-the-Forest. The numerous herbaceous borders within the walled garden are the most impressive feature of this garden.

deal of attention. Neither the lake at the end or the stream that runs down the side of this garden have been exploited in any meaningful way, although they are a haven of wildlife and wild plants.

Hutton-in-the-Forest. Some colour combinations may be unexpected but they work very effectively.

On the walk back up to the west side of the house, one's nose is assailed by the smell of garlic from the acres of ramsons or wild garlic that grow under the trees. However one's attention is diverted as soon as the vast walled garden at the back of the house is entered. This is in fact only walled on two sides, the other two sides, including that in front of the house, are lined by a delightfully irregular yew hedge. Although this garden is basically divided up into four sections by two paths that cross in the middle it is in no way a symmetrical or a formal garden. Indeed until recently it was not a decorative garden at all, but full of lettuces and other kitchen produce. Fortunately it is now being put to better use, although parts of it still need to be given a firmer identity, especially on the north side.

The first section of the main path is bordered by roses, backed by a newly planted yew hedge and underplanted with silver-leaved plants such as clove-scented carnations, santolina, artemisia, nepeta and lavender. On either side of these borders are large areas of grass; one side leading right up to the yew hedge and on the other up to espaliered apples.

Past the central feature of a large copper container surrounded by eight large yew eggs, the path continues, lined now with

91

herbaceous borders, and this time backed with mature yew hedges. Although not over-wide, about 2.5 m (8 ft), the borders have a good mixture of plants including *Thermiopsis*, *Astilbe*, several geraniums (including *G. renardii*, *G. clarkei* 'Kashmir White' and *G. phaeum*), various oriental poppies including the giant red *Papaver orientale* 'Goliath', *Astrantia major* 'Sunningdale Variegated', and *Thalictrum aquilegifolium*. There is also a stand of *Senecio tangutica*, a very attractive plant for late summer with large airy conical heads of small yellow flowers that look as good in seed as they do in flower. However, it does run, so it should only be planted where it has room to spread or where it can be controlled.

At the end of this border the path turns in either direction, parallel to the wall, creating a long border along its length. Other borders are placed on the lawn side of the path and these are cleverly planted with lower plants so that from the lawn, with the path invisible amongst the plants, it looks as though the two borders are one large bed, with the plants increasing in size as they approach the wall. The central part of this border is planted with hotter colours of the reds, yellows and oranges. Plants include *Geum borisii*, *Ligularia* of various sorts, and Bowles' golden grass (*Milium effusum aureum*). There is a good clump of *Smilacina racemosa*, delicately shaded by *Rosa glauca* (*R. rubrifolia*).

The lower border contains several geraniums including the grey-leafed *G. renardii*, the strange star-like flowered *G.* × *oxonianum* 'Thurstonianum' and the wonderful silvery blue-flowered *G. pratense* 'Mrs Kendall Clark'. There are also some nice stands of the pink *Dicentra formosa*. Tucked away at the feet of other plants is the small *Alchemilla conjuncta*, with its neatly pleated, dark green leaves that have a silver edging. This precise little plant, whose flowers can be dried, makes a nice change from its larger relations. Other small plants include various violas.

There is a small border down the second wall, but the only really interesting area is where the two walls meet which includes *Veratrum nigrum*, *Ligularia* 'Desdemona', *Trillium luteum*, a very good stand of *Dicentra spectabilis* with a pink columbine (*Aquilegia vulgaris*) through which climbs *Codonopsis clematidea* with its intriguing bell-shaped flowers.

Along the lawns on this side of the garden are a few frames for climbing roses that look rather odd here; perhaps another herbaceous border would be more in keeping with the existing arrangement, relegating the roses to their own proper rose garden elsewhere. Indeed with the excellence of the existing herbaceous borders it is to be hoped that several other such beds are created turning the whole of this walled garden into one of the best in Cumbria.

After the feast of colour it is nice to be able to stroll in the coolness of the woodland gardens. Again there is much to be done here to bring them back to their former glory, but it all takes time and money and for the moment the trees suffice and one must be grateful for being able to enjoy their magnificence.

Potentially this is one of the most exciting gardens in the Lake District. With time and trouble, as well as imagination, there is so much that can be created not only close to the house, but also in the surrounding areas with their magnificent woods, streams and lakes. A look at the pump garden will show what can be done to create interest in even a small area and the work in the walled garden is equally impressive. One really wonders what this garden will be like in ten years' time if the same kind of imagination and drive continue to be applied.

Hutton-in-the-Forest. Looking down the main path between silver-foliaged plants backed by shrub roses.

19
LEVENS HALL
Near Kendal

(Owned by C. H. Bagot Esq.)

Open: *Easter-end Sept, 11–5. Closed Fri, Sat. £2.50. House also open (same times).*

Directions: *8 km (5 miles) s of Kendal, at junction of A590 and A6. Ample parking.*

Access: *level, with wheelchair ramp at entrance.*

Main attractions: *restored seventeenth-century garden with parterres and topiary, herbaceous and shrub borders, nut plantation.*

Teas: *teashop in house.*

Plants for sale: *from garden, including some rarities.*

Nearby gardens: *Sizergh Castle (27), Dallam Tower (8), Halecat (13).*

THE GARDENS at Levens Hall are some of the best known in the Lake District. This is mainly because of its superb collection of topiary that is undoubtedly the best of its type in the country. In more recent times other areas of the garden have also contributed to its growing reputation.

It is quite remarkable that the garden has come down to us from the end of the seventeenth century in the condition that it has. Most owners of big houses of this type were prone to the fashions of their day in all aspects of their life, and their gardens were no exception. Most gardens have passed through several major changes since parterres and topiary were the thing of the day and on the whole the survival of the latter in this country has been in the hands of the cottage gardener as have so many discarded aspects of gardening. However, through unwillingness to change in the first instance and neglect in the second the gardens at Levens Hall have come down to us, perhaps not quite as their creator might have envisaged, but still as a reasonably accurate account of what they were like.

The origins of Levens Hall go back to the construction of the pele tower in the thirteenth century. Many important changes took place in the early seventeenth century, but it was towards the end of that century when James Grahame took over the estate, that the gardens were developed to what we know today. They were laid out between 1689 and 1710 mainly by a French gardener, Guillaume Beaumont, who had been trained by the famous André le Nôtre at Versailles. Planting plans still exist and show that the gardens, in particular the parterre, are as they were created. Grahame's daughter, who inherited the Hall, was impressed by Beaumont and his work and refused to allow it to be altered during her lifetime. Thereafter it fell into neglect until it was restored in the nineteenth century, reputedly with 14.5 km (9 miles) of box hedging required to replace that which had become hopelessly overgrown.

The first garden, however, that the visitor enters has only recently been laid out. This is a recreation of a seventeenth-century garden, using only plants that were known to be in cultivation before 1700. Perhaps one could imagine that these may be wizened old plants with little of the flower-power that has been bred into modern cultivars, but, in fact, most of them are familiar to anyone who gardens at the end of the twentieth century. Some are what we would recognize as herbs still in use today, such as chives (*Allium schoenoprasum*), while others we rarely have need for, wolf's bane (*Aconitum napellus*) for example. Others, *Smilacina racemosa* and *Doronicum* for instance, are now grown for pure decoration. All the plants in these borders have been labelled although one or two labels have outlived their plants. English names are given, occasionally in rather bizarre forms; for example *Eryngium alpinum* is given as 'Alpine sea holly'. Although one understands what is meant, mountain sea plants are a strange concept!

Moving around to the front of the house one is confronted with a

Levens Hall. This garden is rightly known for its magnificent topiary, underplanted with a variety of bedding plants.

vast walled lawn with just a trace of plantings down the side. The scale creates a calm and dignified approach to the house and certainly acts as a wonderful contrast to what the visitor is about to witness. Modern man is so used to being entertained that a lawn of these proportions to many visitors must seem boring and a waste of an opportunity for creating rose gardens or mixed borders, but an area of tranquillity is essential to such a garden as this.

Passing through the gateway at the side of the house takes the visitor into the parterre which is about as tranquil as a stormy sea. Here there are low box hedges enclosing small beds of different shapes, with narrow paths in between. The beds are filled with spring bedding, followed by summer bedding. They form a colourful patchwork, sometimes bright, sometimes more subdued with pastel colours. Some beds are confined to one variety, white tulips or yellow pansies in spring or *Verbena* 'Silver Anne' in summer, for example, while others are a mixture of plants. Massed bedding is difficult to handle and can come to resemble the worst of municipal plantings if care is not taken. Here it generally works marvellously.

The parterre in itself is not particularly unique, but the topiary that also rises from these beds is. Most of it dates back to the seventeenth century, although it is possible that some were replaced during the restoration in the nineteenth century. Some are clipped into geometric shapes, others into figurative ones. Many have rather endearing names, such as 'Judge's Wig', 'The Howard Lion', 'Queen Elizabeth and Her Maids of Honour' or the large 'Umbrella Tree'. The whole of this large garden is a seething mass of topiary, some a little out of shape, but none the worse for that.

It is interesting to stand and speculate as to how the garden looked soon after it had been planted and the impatience there must have been to see the results, and then gradually the trees mature and suddenly appear to have been there for ever. A romantic notion, perhaps, but it is an experience most gardeners have had, especially with yew which one is always told will take an age. In fact it is relatively quick growing and few can have regretted planting it instead of some faster growing shrub. One should never worry about how far away future maturity is; never take short cuts, because it is surprising how fast time passes. Even the youngest gardens soon develop to their full potential. Having said that, of course it does take two or three centuries to produce yews of this maturity! Some of the smaller pieces of topiary are of box (*Buxus sempervirens*) but this is no faster growing than yew.

There is more to see in this area besides the parterres and the topiary, especially around the walls. At the narrower end of the garden there are borders containing a variety of herbaceous plants and shrubs as well as climbers on the walls. In one corner an ancient wisteria climbs 15 m (50 ft) or more up into a lime tree. Another interesting plant against this wall is *Ribes speciosum* with its bright red, fuchsia-like flowers, hanging against a dark green foliage. This is perhaps a plant that should be seen more frequently. In this area the planting of the parterre is not confined to bedding as some of the beds also contain roses.

Before leaving this garden it is worth looking at the yew hedge at the far end of it. In this grows a most splendid display of *Tropaeolum speciosum*, a perennial nasturtium. This is a feature that has been adopted all over the Lake District, but nowhere will you see it to such effect as on this tall hedge.

If this were all there were to see at Levens the visitor would have had his or her money's worth, but there is more, perhaps not so spectacular, but still worth looking at. Much of it is still being developed. The broad path on the far side of the Topiary Garden continues down the length of the garden and its sheltering wall presents the opportunity for a long border that is filled with interesting shrubs as it seemingly disappears to the horizon. From this broad path there are further paths leading to several interesting gardens. The first leads across grass towards the herb garden, where a plantation of nuts has recently been planted. The herb garden itself contains all manner of interesting plants including hostas and a splendid clump of the giant rhubarb, *Rheum palmatum*. Time spent browsing here would be well spent.

The next garden along is the old orchard. Between this and the beech hedge is a small herbaceous garden that is slowly being added to. Some plants are already forming large clumps, there being a particularly fine stand of *Ligularia* 'The Rocket' for example, which makes an eye-catching display in summer.

Further along the broad path, just beyond the orchard, one comes to the main herbaceous borders which stretch down to the beech hedge and continue on the other side down to the ha-ha, the boundary of the garden. These borders are full of a wide range of herbaceous plants, far too numerous to name, from the common *Alchemilla mollis* to the less familiar *Senecio tangutica* with its large conical heads of small yellow flowers. These have an airy quality about them as do the seed heads that follow. It is an attractive plant and is particularly useful as it flowers in late summer and autumn; however, it has got a nasty habit of running.

The borders are bisected by a very tall beech hedge in the form of a roundel with two avenues stretching away at right angles. These are also the work of Guillaume Beaumont although whether he had envisaged them as becoming so impressively tall is unknown. It is also doubtful that when he planted them he foresaw that these vast structures would become home to a dense ribbon of wild garlic (*Allium ursinum*) stretching across the garden in spring. A wonderful sight as long as they stay confined to the hedge.

Beyond the herbaceous borders is a large sunken lawn. The border at the top of the bank alongside the wide path is a silver border, edged on the lawn side by nepeta. This is obviously a dry and sunny position and will suit silver-leaved plants well.

Unusually for a garden in the Lake District, Levens Hall does not have any water features, natural or otherwise. However, there is so much else to see that this is of no consequence. A garden with so much topiary can never be dull and with the addition of both the spring and summer bedding, and the herbaceous borders, there is much to see and enjoy.

Levens Hall. Several of the tall yew hedges are planted with the bright red, climbing nasturtium, *Tropaeolum speciosum*.

20
LINGHOLM

Near Keswick

(Owned by Viscount Rochdale)

RHODODENDRONS are as much part of the Lake District as they are of the Himalayas, and never more so than here at Lingholm. The same could also be said about meconopsis and primulas. The garden is in ideal position for growing all these plants as it has a natural acid soil, the site is protected by the hills and existing vegetation, especially the oak trees, and it has a high rainfall providing it with a damp atmosphere.

In terms of most of the other larger houses mentioned in this book, Lingholm is relatively new. It was built in the 1870s for a Colonel Greenall. The gardens were not laid out until early in the twentieth century when the house was owned by another Colonel, George Kemp, later to become Lord Rochdale. In the intervening period the house was let out for summer hire and for several years Beatrix Potter's family rented it and it was here that *The Tale of Squirrel Nutkin* was written. Once the terraces and other gardens had been laid out the collection of rhododendrons and azaleas was started and were mainly introduced in the 1920s and 1930s.

The gardens are in a wonderful position on the shores of Derwent Water with good views of the fells all around. The gardens are vast, taking in large sweeps of the woodland that stretches in low hills, protected by the towering Catbells, Causey Pike and Barrow. Closer to the house are more intimate areas which contain more conventional plantings. It is a garden in which there is much to enjoy and in which one can linger.

The car park is set part way down the drive but the stroll up to the reception area is well taken up by looking at the mature trees that line it, including, just inside the gate, a magnificent fern-leaved beech *Fagus sylvatica* 'Aspleniifolia'. On the right where the drive forks is a majestic *Cedrus atlantica glauca*, not a tree for a small

Open: *most of the year, 1 April–31 Oct, 10–5, £2.20 (accompanied children free).*

Directions: *w side of Derwent Water, near head of lake. Ample parking a little way from garden.*

Access: *full tour involves a lot of walking, but paths in good condition. Wheelchair access to most areas.*

Main attractions: *rhododendrons, extensive woodland, herbaceous borders, mature specimen trees.*

Teas: *tearoom with veranda; light lunches also served.*

Plants for sale: *good selection of rhododendrons and other plants from garden in small nursery beside tearoom; glasshouse sells indoor plants.*

Nearby gardens: *Fellside (10), Palace Howe (22).*

garden. In front of the reception area is a *Parrotia persica*, sometimes known as the iron tree. This has very good autumn colours and is noted for its winter flowering, the flowers being noticeable for their clusters of red stamens.

The area immediately outside the reception and tearooms is worth examining closely as there are some very interesting shrubs and herbaceous plants here; indeed if this were a garden of a small house then the owner could be justifiably pleased with it. Among the shrubs is *Hoheria lyallii* with its glistening white flowers in mid summer. Nearby is a good bush of the unusual *Daphne acutiloba*, which has white flowers, also produced around mid summer followed by bright red berries. Next to this is the late-flowering *Rhododendron macranthum* (also known as *R. indicum*). Not far away is another daphne, *D. retusa*, a magnificent specimen. Among the herbaceous plants are *Selinum tenuifolium*, a cow parsley relative grown mainly for its delicate filigree leaves; the double meadow-sweet, *Filipendula ulmaria* 'Flore Pleno', the new yellow penstemon *P. pinifolius* 'Mersea Yellow', a low-growing plant with small, fine leaves and narrow yellow trumpets. There is also the annual pea with greenish yellow flowers that is becoming popular, *Lathyrus chlorantha*. Earlier in the season there is the blue-flowered comfrey *Symphytum asperum* which is not such a thug as some of its relatives.

Moving past the greenhouses and the house the visitor enters the garden proper by passing through an attractive gate into Bryony's Garden, a memorial garden. This is only a small garden, but it is rather delightful with a lily pond in the centre and plantings of shrubs and perennial plants around it, chosen to give all-year-round interest. There is a small rock garden on which heathers grow. *Tropaeolum speciosum* is planted to cover these with its flame-red flowers from summer onwards. One of the most unusual and attractive plantings here is *Scrophularia aquatica* 'Variegata', a figwort with its pale green leaves edged with cream variegations, through which grows *Primula* 'Inverewe', the mealy stems and calyces echoing the variegation of the figwort, and setting off the bright orange flowers.

Leaving by another individual gate, this time with doves above it, one comes to the terrace and the main herbaceous plantings. The border here is split up into five main sections, each delineated by a low hedge of variegated box. The central and main sections are devoted to dwarf rhododendrons, at their best in late spring. These are all clearly labelled, as indeed are all the other plants in the garden. The other sections are filled with herbaceous plants of various sorts that give a long season from the *Trollius* in spring until

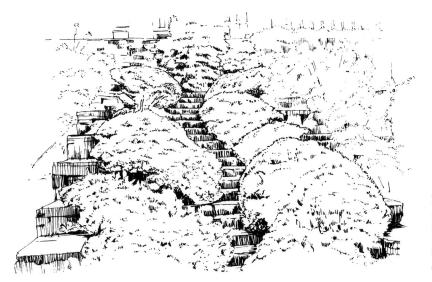

Lingholm. The attractive steps down to the main lawn have become progressively narrower as the clumps of heather spread.

the *Kirengeshoma* in late autumn. Many of the plants are those that will appreciate the moist climate here. Thus there are good stands of *Meconopsis chelidoniifolia* and *M.* × *beamishii*, as well as the more commonly seen *Nepeta govaniana*.

As well as good colour combinations there are some very good associations of foliage. For example at the southern end of the border there is a lovely planting of the plume poppy, *Macleaya cordata*, with its feathery flowers and glaucous, fingered foliage; *Astilboides tabularis*, with its large round leaves, and the delicate strap-like leaves of the short pampas grass *Cortaderia selloana* 'Pumila'. The wall behind the border, supporting the terrace above, is obviously quite warm in winter as there are several plants trained against it that are usually considered relatively tender. For example there is *Jasminum* × *stephanense, Cytisus battandieri, Schisandra rubrifolia* and *Sophora tetraptera* 'Goughensis', the last being the most tender. At the northern end of the border, the one nearest the memorial garden, there is a clump of bulbs of a type that is not frequently seen. This is the summer-flowering *Notholirion bulbuliferum*. It has lavender-blue flowers with green tips to the petals. The flower heads can be up to 90 cm (3 ft) from the ground and include up to twenty-five or more individual flowers.

Opposite the middle of the border is a flight of steps leading down to a lawn. These steps are edged on either side with hummocks of heather, just leaving an irregular narrow path down which to descend. The border against the terrace is lined with the white *Rhododendron yunnanense* alternating with buddleja, one for the late spring and the other for the late summer. The lawn is surrounded by trees and shrubs including some fine acers.

Leaving this part of the garden through the gate at the southern end of the terrace, the visitor passes under another splendid

Lingholm. Fine contrasts in the shape of foliage are to be found in the herbaceous borders.

example of the fern-leaved beech, *Fagus sylvatica* 'Aspleniifolia', which seems to do so well in the Lake District. The path turns right and passes beside private areas of the garden towards the woodland areas. On the left is a large meadow in which daffodils flower in spring. There is also an avenue of pink flowering cherries that adds a touch of gaiety to the dull grey sky of a wet spring day.

The path passes through a strip of trees and shrubs before it gets to the drive past the cottages. There are several trees of note here. In particular, on the right, an *Embothrium coccineum* which has bright flame-red flowers over a long period in early summer, and on the left an unusual rowan, *Sorbus mitchellii* with its enormous rounded leaves. Another curious thing about the latter is that its grafted trunk is much fatter than the rootstock on which it stands. The route leads on past the cottages, against the walls of which in sum-mer is a blaze of orange *Kniphofia* 'Shining Sceptre'. The display indicates that this plant's need for full sun is well met.

One soon leaves the drive and starts to follow paths, first of all through a new planting, that lead on for several miles through the woods. Here one is really in rhododendron country and could well be in the Himalayas, especially on a day when low cloud drifts through the trees. Luckily the rhododendrons do not flower all at the same time so there is a long period from early spring to early summer when there will always be something in flower. Another point is that when you have such a large number of different species and hybrids there is always bound to be a fascinating variation in the shape and texture of the plant and its leaves.

The woods are not confined to rhododendrons and azaleas. Towards the far end of the walk the visitor is suddenly confronted with a large patch of the blue poppy, *Meconopsis betonicifolia*, another touch of the Himalayas. A further reminder are the primulas that frequently border the path. Also at the far end is a boggy valley which is filled with yellow azaleas *Rhododendron luteum* that produce a superb scent when they are in flower. Common these azaleas may be, but what wonderful plants they are. Needless to say many of the rhododendrons are not common and walking through these woods introduces the visitor to a wide range of unusual varieties.

Back at the reception area there is a good tearoom for a welcome cup of tea and a small nursery where quite a number of rhododendrons can be purchased. If time is limited in the Lake District then this is one of the gardens that should be seen. Although late spring and early summer is the peak for the rhododendrons, summer is good for the herbaceous plants and autumn for coloured foliage — an all-year-round garden.

Lingholm. Pieris grows well in the Lake District as can be seen here with this specimen of *P. formosa forrestii* 'Wakehurst'.

21
MUNCASTER CASTLE
Near Ravenglass

(Owned by Mr and Mrs Patrick Gordon-Duff-Pennington)

Open: *most of the year, 11–5 (including Owl Centre). £2.80. House open April–Oct except Mon.*

Directions: *on A595 coast road, just E of Ravenglass. Large car park opposite entrance plus limited parking near gate for nursery only.*

Access: *hilly terrain but much of garden can be viewed from level drive and paths.*

Main attractions: *rhododendrons, 1 km (⅔ mile) long terrace, secret garden, Owl Centre.*

Teas: *tearoom which also serves light lunches. Outside seating.*

Plants for sale: *attached nursery stocks rhododendrons, shrubs, alpines, herbaceous. Nearby Boonwood Garden Centre specializes in indoor plants.*

THE LAKE DISTRICT is very rich in gardens that specialize in rhododendrons, mainly because of the suitability of the climate and soil conditions, but also partly because of the presence of Muncaster, which provided both the inspiration and much of the material to get many of the others started. This garden has been a place of rhododendron pilgrimage for most of the current century and looks set to continue into the next.

Muncaster Castle owes its existence to its commanding views over the Eskdale valley. However, it was not the beauty of the views that its earliest builders, the Romans, appreciated but its defensive position. Part of the subsequent castle that was built on the site of the fort was erected during the thirteenth century, but it is mainly the late nineteenth-century additions that we see today.

The present garden really stems from the year 1917, when Sir John Ramsden inherited the estate. The mild, moist climate which Muncaster enjoys, mainly because of the warming influence of the sea, which in turn is warmed by the Gulf Stream, along with its acid soil conditions, means that it is ideal for growing rhododendrons. Sir John already had a large collection of these shrubs at his garden at Balstrude in Buckinghamshire and once he had taken over Muncaster from the last Duke he set about moving many of them to his new home. He took shares in various plant hunting expeditions of the period including important ones by Frank Kingdon-Ward and later by Ludlow and Sherriff. In return for his part in financing the trips he received a good deal of seed of rhododendron species, many new to cultivation. These were raised and planted out in the gardens. They also became the basis for his breeding programme in which he raised his own hybrids. Many of these are still to be seen in the gardens and a few such as *R.* 'Muncaster Mist' and *R.* 'Blue Haze' are still available from nurseries.

The garden at Muncaster is very extensive, which ensures the visitor plenty of exercise although, fortunately, most of it can be seen without leaving reasonably flat ground. There are two possible entrances, one is from the car park opposite the main gates while the other is from the much smaller car park next to the nursery, which is primarily meant for visitors buying plants. Apart from having to cross the road, the former is the best way of entering the gardens as it means you can take a leisurely walk up the length of the drive from which a major part of the rhododendron collection can be easily seen.

The drive winds through a long valley and both sides are clothed with trees and rhododendrons. This is an ideal situation for them as they are not only protected from the cold and strong winds, but also from the strong sun. By the amount of lichen around the air must be fairly pure here, another similarity to the rhododendron's home of the Himalayas. The walk along this valley can be quite magical, especially if you can time it so that there are no other visitors present. However, there are bound to be plenty of birds around, a feature of so many Lakeland gardens, and your journey is likely to be accompanied by sounds of rooks.

The land rises up on either side of the drive and is dominated by huge trees, mainly conifers and beech. Nestling beneath these are all manner of rhododendrons and azaleas. An alternative path goes off to the left that gives the visitor an even closer look at some of the plants. It runs parallel to the main drive and rejoins it before the main gardens are reached.

Also running beside the drive is a small stream. At the point where the valley widens out this is lined with *Lysichiton americanum*, often known as the skunk cabbage because of its foetid smell. The curious flower, which appears in spring, is a short yellow spike, surrounded by a yellow spathe. The leaves which initially look a bit like a those of a cos lettuce, are held upright and get larger and larger until they are 120–150 cm (4–5 ft) tall — not something to introduce into a small garden, especially as it has a tendency to spread. Also along this stream are clumps of candelabra primulas, such as *P. japonica*.

On rounding the final bend, you will see the pink stone of the castle. Surprisingly there are no gardens in the conventional sense near the building although there are the occasional plantings of hydrangeas on banks, or astilbes and primulas near wildfowl ponds. As you near the castle, the gash in the hillside known as

Muncaster Ghyll comes into view. From the terrace this valley appears quite dramatic as the visitor looks down onto and across at the rounded hummocks that are large bushes and the tops of trees. In late spring and early summer this is one of the highlights of the garden, since many of these trees and shrubs are rhododendrons along with a scattering of magnolia and camellias. As can be imagined the combined effect can be stunning, especially as the ghyll opens up into the broad valley of the river Esk with views of the fells beyond.

Turning away from the house and crossing the northern tip of the ghyll the visitor enters the beginning of the terrace. With everything on a grand scale in this garden the fact that this is a good half a mile long should come as no surprise. It is not only its length that makes this part of the garden worth visiting. It follows the contour of the hill and has incredible views across the river valley below and way up into the fells beyond. The sounds of river life echo up from below to this privileged view point. The promenader is separated from the view by a box hedge, low enough just to see over, which runs the full length of the terrace. It is punctuated at regular intervals with buttresses of yew that give the

Muncaster Castle. As well as plenty of rhododendrons and other interesting trees and shrubs, there are spectacular views to be seen from various parts of the garden.

Muncaster Castle. A delightful rustic summer house overlooking the valley from the long terrace.

whole thing a castellated effect, almost like a castle wall. Every other yew is a golden one. This is not so noticeable in spring, but once the new growth commences they are suffused with a wonderful golden glow.

The terrace itself is a broad strip of close-mown grass. This is backed by innumerable trees and shrubs of a wide range of species and varieties. Amongst many other things there are a number of acers, pieris, tree heathers, hebes, berberis, magnolias and of course, rhododendrons, sometimes in profusion. About a third of the way along the terrace is a rustic summer house, almost surrounded by acers. It is now in need of repair, but in its heyday it must have been a sheer delight to sit here and look across the

107

valley. Behind the summer house are various camellias and rhododendrons through which paths lead to a churchyard gate. Another, similar summer house is found at the far end of the terrace. The shrubs and trees at this end of the terrace tend to include more native species. The underplanting of the shrubs along the terrace is very informal; drifts of daffodils (*Narcissus*), Solomon's seal (*Polygonatum* × *hybridum*), bluebells (*Hyacinthoides non-scripta*), foxgloves (*Digitalis purpurea*) and lily of the valley (*Convallaria majalis*) vie with other native flora. This is an altogether delightful place to stroll.

Once back at the castle there are all the woodlands on the far side of it to explore. Although the predominant feature is again rhododendrons, there are many other interesting trees and shrubs to look at. Amongst these are a fine collection of southern beeches, *Nothofagus*. These are wonderful trees, which are unfortunately not seen very frequently in this country as many of the species are somewhat tender. Fortunately the climate here at Muncaster allows them to flourish. Spectacular flowering is not restricted to the rhododendrons nor to the spring. *Eucryphia* with their dish-like white flowers, decoratively filled with a boss of stamens, also thrive, as well as the spectacular handkerchief tree, *Davidia involucrata*, with its large white bracts that flutter in the wind.

There is much else to see at Muncaster besides the gardens. There is a famous owl centre which houses one of the largest collections of owls in the world. It is also the Headquarters of the British Owl Breeding and Release Scheme. There are many other events that are of more particular interest to gardeners. In spring, walks and lectures on rhododendrons are arranged and in autumn there is a propagation weekend.

Another feature is the nursery which, as one would expect, is strong in rhododendrons. It is housed in the old walled kitchen garden. Beyond the main glasshouse is a small secret garden which basically consists of paths winding through conifers, heathers and evergreen shrubs. Every so often one comes across a surprise planting and daffodils (*Narcissus* 'Sun Disk' for example) or lilies. It shows what can be done in a small space.

Muncaster presents a good opportunity for seeing a great number of rhododendrons without having to mount a Himalayan-style expedition. The garden has been a bit neglected in recent times. Many trees and shrubs are getting old and are in need of attention. New planting and rejuvenation are also needed if it is to go into the next century in good heart. Fortunately this is beginning to happen.

22
PALACE HOW

Brackenthwaite, near Loweswater

(Owned by Mr and Mrs A. & K. Johnson)

PALACE HOW is one of those gardens whose apparent simplicity belies all the thought and work that has gone into it. The layout is immediately comprehensible even though it cannot all be seen at a glance. The positions of the beds, backed by an oak wood on one side and the soaring fells on the other, are well thought out and would probably look good even if they were restricted to rhododendrons and nothing else, but this is a garden of some character and this character is as much to do with the plants in it as it is with the way they are laid out.

With some gardens it is difficult to imagine that they have ever been anything else than a garden, but they have all had to start somewhere and often, like this one, they started as a piece of field, in this case a boggy one. From this blank canvas of about an acre, a garden has been created in a relatively short space of time. For those that have the daunting challenge of starting a garden from scratch it is invaluable to have the opportunity to wander round a garden like this to see what has been done and how it has been achieved. Here, as well as a rough field, the owners have had to contend with very wet and cold conditions, but the plants they grow show how they have put this to advantage, working with nature rather than against it.

The basis of the garden is a big irregular lawn surrounded and intruded into by beds and borders. This large lawn creates a feeling of spaciousness, particularly where it wanders off behind shrubs and yet it has an intimacy, in part created by the surrounding fells and woods which enclose it. It is not a level lawn, but one that undulates slightly, following the lie of the land, a good thing to do in this area where any flat surface looks out of character.

The planting varies considerably in height from ground-hugging

Open: limited: see Yellow Book and local press.

Directions: Lorton Vale, 10 km (6 miles) SE of Cockermouth. From B5289 N of Crummock Water, garden well signposted when open. Parking in adjacent field; parking for disabled nearer house.

Access: mostly level; wheelchair access.

Main attractions: scree beds, meconopsis, shrubs and trees, plantings suitable to cold, damp area.

Teas: Barn tearooms, New House Farm 1.5 km (1 mile) away towards Lorton: light lunches and excellent home-made cream teas.

Plants for sale: some plants grown in garden.

Nearby gardens: nearest is Lingholm (20).

alpines to trees, all giving an important three-dimensional quality. The alpines are mainly grown in a couple of scree beds adjacent to the house. The purpose of growing them here is two-fold. In the first place it is sensible to have low-growing plants in front of the windows, particularly if you spend a great deal of time in the kitchen, so that you can see over them and not have your view blocked by larger plants. The second point is that alpines tend to be small plants that need to be looked at closely to be appreciated. Being near to the house they are easy to observe whereas a rhododendron, for example, can be placed at a distance and can still be enjoyed even if there is not time (or if it is too wet) to go close up to it.

These alpine beds have the disadvantage of being at the bottom of a slope which means they get wet, but one is built over a sand pit making the drainage acute and both have raised areas which keep many of the plants above the surrounding wet soil. There are

Palace How. One of the delights of this garden is the number of self-sown meconopsis that shine out of the borders.

some wonderful plants in these beds and it is worth spending a while looking at them in detail before you wander off to the rest of the garden.

Palace How. This garden contains some of the most interesting and colourful alpines to be seen in the area.

Anemone trullifolia, with small buttercup flowers of blue, is a very unusual plant, but does well here in slight shade and moist ground. There are several daphnes, both in these beds and elsewhere in the garden, which are not only pleasing to the eye but also add a wonderful fragrance to the garden. Several New Zealand plants are to be seen here, which is a good choice for a moist garden as alpines from this country are often permanently surrounded by mists and damp ground. Two species of *Aciphylla*, *Celmisia*, *Geranium sessiliflorum novaezealandiae* 'Nigricans' and dwarf hebes are amongst them. The first are strange and unusual plants with spiky leaves that make weeding near them a hazardous business. The geranium, in spite of its long name, is a delightful little plant with brown leaves and small white flowers that gently self-sows about.

Other plants of interest include *Phlox* 'Chattahoochee', *Sorbus reducta*, the silver-foliaged *Euryops acraeus* from southern Africa which has bright yellow daisy-like flowers in profusion, the piercingly bright *Geranium cinereum subcaulescens*, *Dryas octopetala* and a magnificent carpet of *Lithodora diffusa* 'Heavenly Blue'. Further alpines and low-growing plants are grown in these beds and in the area immediately outside the alpine house (into which you can peer

111

but not enter). Beside the alpine house is a raised bed of silver-leaved plants. These plants generally will not thrive in damp or shady conditions and the use of a raised, well-drained bed in an area of high rainfall is about the only way of growing them successfully.

Having passed between the two alpine beds onto the lawn, one is immediately drawn towards the pond. This is a delightful feature. The planting is not over-ambitious and yet it is very effective indeed. Herbaceous plants (including *Rodgersia* and *Hosta*) and shrubs, build up into a backdrop at the far end, with the bank on the left being covered with dwarf rhododendrons, under small trees such as birch (*Betula*). Near the water's edge grow a profusion of candelabra primulas including *P. japonica* and the mealy-stemmed *P. pulverulenta*. The other two sides open onto the lawn, although edged with various plants, including more primulas and clumps of *Iris sibirica*. Dotted here and there amongst the plants are various species of *Meconopsis*. In a bed to the right of the pond there are even more. They love the damp conditions here and self-sow happily around. Of all the gardens open to the public in the Lakes this has one of the best displays (although not necessarily the most plants) and it is well worth visiting for these alone. Visitors from the south in particular will feel envious of the way they grow, given the right conditions. The blue flowers look just perfect and will shine out of the shadier spots like beacons. I especially like those that are backed by the purple leaves of an acer. Not only are there blues, but also a white *M. betonicifolia* and a beautiful yellow *M. integrifolia*.

Shrubs and trees are a dominant feature of this garden. Many are quite common, especially the acers, conifers and rhododendrons, which abound in this part of the world (yet they are none the worse for this), but many are much rarer and it is well worth walking round, especially the paths behind the beds, looking at what there is dotted about. *Halesia tetraptera* (*H. carolina*) with its pure white bells hanging from the branches is one to look out for. Another white-flowered shrub worth spotting is *Staphylea colchica*. A curious member of the yew family that can be seen is *Sciadopitys verticillata*. As yet this is only a very young plant, but it can eventually grow as high as 36 m (120 ft). (Visitors in a hundred years' time should find this a rather dominant plant in this garden, if it has not out-grown its welcome by then!)

Another tree of interest, especially as it is ideal for a damp garden is the alder *Alnus glutinosa* 'Imperialis' with its finely cut leaves. A shrub for these conditions is *Salix daphnoides* which has dark stems that are covered with a white bloom. This can become a tall tree unless it is regularly pollarded as here.

It is not only the shrubs that are unusual as there are many rarer herbaceous and perennial plants in the various beds. The woodlander *Jeffersonia dubia* with its beautiful bluey purple flowers is tucked away with the meconopsis. Another woodlander that is hidden at the back of some of the beds is *Veratrum nigrum*. As a contrast there are several plants of *Pulsatilla alpina apiifolia* with their beautiful sulphur yellow flowers dominating the front of the beds at the time when the garden is open. There are several other pulsatillas. Ground cover is provided amongst others by *Tiarella cordifolia* with its soft spikes of creamy flowers and by the sub-shrub *Cornus canadensis* which has white bracts around the green flowers. The flowers of both plants are useful for lighting up gloomy spots in the shade under trees and shrubs.

This then is a garden in which to revel. Take your time when walking round, look into every part of the garden as you are bound to find something new. In spite of its size, there are more plants here of interest to the keen gardener than in many of the bigger gardens with their more park-like approach. When you have been round, turn about and go round the other way, you are likely to find even more things that you missed first time. Nearly all the plants are labelled, but Mrs Johnson will more than willingly answer any questions that you may have.

23
RANNERDALE COTTAGE

Crummock Water, north of Buttermere

(Owned by the McElney family)

Open: *under National Gardens Scheme (see Yellow Book). 80p.*

Directions: *on B5289 where it skirts E side of Crummock Water. Well signposted when garden is open. Ample parking in nearby field.*

Access: *generally level with occasional steps.*

Main attractions: *compact garden encompassing many features in clever design.*

Teas: *served in garden; also Barn tearooms — see Palace How (22).*

Plants for sale: *no.*

Nearby gardens: *nearest is Lingholm (20).*

ONE FEATURE that all the gardens in this book have in common is that none of them can be taken in at a glance, no matter how small they are. This is one of the smallest, if not the smallest and yet this principle still holds true. It takes almost as long to get round this garden as it does some that are several times its size.

In spite of its small size this garden seems to have everything: lawns, terraces, a very active stream, secret gardens, a summer house, a peaceful woodland area, a pond, herbaceous plants, plenty of trees and shrubs, and even a functional herb garden. How it is possible to cram all this into less than half an acre without it looking a mess or over-stuffed has to be seen to be believed. Another feature is that it seems to be on several different levels in spite of it being basically a flat garden. Visiting Rannerdale Cottage is a good education on how to construct a small garden, as well as an enjoyable experience.

The cottage does have certain advantages that many would envy. In front, Crummock Water stretches away into the distance towards Loweswater, and behind and to either side (and on the far side of the lake for that matter), the fells rise steeply, encircling it in their embrace. Both Grasmoor, the highest at 852 m (2800 ft) with Lad Hows in front, and Whiteless Peak 660 m (2200 ft) seem to rise straight out of the garden. With such a dramatic position, creating an effective garden becomes a difficult task.

With the possible exception of the stream that runs down one side of the garden, there are probably no straight lines in this garden, everything leads sinuously from one area to another. Immediately behind the house is a lawn from which everything else ultimately flows. From here paths lead off in all directions with borders in between. Around the lawn, as well as numerous shrubs, there are various cottage garden-type lilies such as *L. martagon* and *L. pyrenaicum*. Other noticeable features here are the clumps of peonies. There is a dark pink *Lavatera olbia*, which is echoed nearby by a similarly coloured *Sidalcea*. A deceased apple tree carries the spreading arms of *Clematis tangutica* 'Bill Mackenzie'. Another, still alive and bearing apples, is embraced by a vigorous rose that is outlined against the fells beyond; a good use of vertical space in a small garden.

From the lawn, near a good specimen of *Magnolia* × *soulangeana*, a path covered in stone chippings leads through shrubs into a circular rose garden. This has a bird bath in the middle and four quadrants of a low-growing rose. This is possibly the geographic centre of the garden, and from the circular path, surrounded by shrubs, further paths lead off in all directions. One leads up to a terrace outside a large summer house. Behind the terrace is a steep drop into the stream that rushes down from the fells above. This stream continues down one side of the garden to a wonderful area tucked away in a corner which consists of tall pine trees, with longish grass underneath, and a simple wooden seat. In spite of the proximity of the road this is a peaceful place, uncluttered with

Rannerdale Cottage. A tranquil cottage garden bordering a lake and over-topped by fells.

vegetation as the branches are cut high on the trunks and there is no other planting. It is good to have such a tranquil place in a garden which is otherwise so full.

Back into the main garden the visitor continues to ramble though the maze of paths, sometimes passing under rose arches, often through shrubs. The stream is left unadorned as there is no waterside planting at all, but a trickle of water is piped off to feed a small pool near the house in which goldfish constantly play. Here there are some water plants, including marginals such as *Caltha palustris*, the kingcup. Behind the magnolia, the centre of the garden is dominated by a tall variegated poplar, *Populus* × *candicans* 'Aurora'. Although near the centre of the Lake District, this garden is obviously not too cold as the variegated *Phormium tenax* readily survives, adding a touch of the exotic to the garden. Another New Zealander that is on the tender side but survives here, is a red-flowered *Leptospermum*, growing against the dry-stone wall. As well as the poplar and the phormium other interesting variegated plants can be found tucked away all over the garden. For example, under a *Lavatera* 'Barnsley' near the summer house is *Geranium macrorrhizum* 'Variegatum' and near the rose garden is a very intriguing *Cornus nuttallii* 'Gold Spot', a tall shrub with typical small flowers of this genus, surrounded by white bracts that last over a long period. This form is distinguished by leaves splashed with gold.

With so many shrubs around, many of the herbaceous plants are those that can cope not only with the more shady positions, but also cope visually with the shapes of the bushes. Thus there are a number of hostas and bergenias as well as the strap-like leaves of hemerocallis. *Pachysandra terminalis* also does well in these conditions and here is represented as another plant in its variegated form. As with so many gardens in this area meconopsis is represented; the red *M. napaulensis* is grown as well as the ubiquitous *M. cambrica*.

Near the kitchen door is a raised bed that is appropriately furnished with a wide range of culinary herbs.

As one moves around the garden there are constant glimpses of the fells above and the glistening water of the lake beyond the road. The garden is strong enough to take in these views as part of the garden and not something to distract the eye. It is a delightful small garden and one that should please all its visitors.

24
RYDAL HALL
Rydal, near Ambleside

(Leased by the Diocese of Carlisle)

THE ONE MAN who had most influence on the larger gardens in the Lake District was Thomas Mawson. He ran a nursery and landscape design business from Windermere and worked on the design of several of the gardens in the area before his reputation spread and he was commissioned for work elsewhere in Britain as well as abroad. In spite of his spreading fame he still undertook local work and in about 1909 he designed the formal gardens at Rydal Hall, then still a private residence.

It is thought that there has been a house of sorts on this site since the beginning of the seventeenth century, but most of the building as seen today stems from the eighteenth and nineteenth centuries. At that time it was at the centre of a thriving estate, but in the twentieth century it has become, in turn, a hotel, a school and finally a conference centre and retreat house for the Diocese of Carlisle. When the Diocese took over, the house was not in the best of repair and time and effort have been spent on it. Once this was achieved, attention was turned to restoring the garden. Much has been achieved, but there is still plenty to do.

The visitor's first view of the garden is an aerial one as you approach it from the terrace around the house. Below is seen a formal garden with precise elements, such as the columnar yews and the geometric beds, set against the natural rolling woodland and fells on the other side of the valley. The contrast is strong and does a lot for the garden.

The way down to the garden is from the centre of the terrace where a double set of stairs descends to a wide central path that bisects the rectangular garden. In the centre is a large circular pool with a fountain which has recently (1984) been restored to working order. Further paths go round the outside of the garden, providing

Open: *9–dusk most days. Free but donations welcomed.*

Directions: *3 km (2 miles) N of Ambleside. Take signposted lane off A591. Parking in drive or nearby.*

Access: *many steep steps, but formal garden can be viewed from top terrace.*

Main attractions: *formal gardens on several levels, woodland ravine, grotto.*

Teas: *numerous teashops in Grasmere.*

Plants for sale: *no.*

Nearby gardens: *Rydal Mount (25), Dove Cottage (9).*

Rydal Hall. In front of the Hall a formal garden creates a feeling of peace and tranquillity.

for a deep 3.6 m (12 ft) border against the retaining wall of the terrace. The two halves of the central portion of the garden are laid down to grass, with a circular bed in the centre of each and further beds in each of the eight corners. These beds are surrounded by low box hedges. The circular ones currently have bedding in them and the corner ones roses. There are columns of yew in each of the corners as well as a further four around the central path where it circles the fountain. In the centre of each of the two circular beds and next to each of the corner ones is an urn on a plinth.

All other planting and points of interest are concentrated in the main border on the house side of the garden and along the south side where a balustrade separates it from the steep drop down to the lower drive. A double stairway, balancing the one on the other side of the garden, leads down to this level. On both sides of the garden there are arbours created by stone columns supporting wooden lintels which in turn support climbing roses that shade the wooden seats below. The large bed below the house is an herbaceous border containing a mixture of fairly familiar plants (but none the worse for that). The dark stone wall is covered with climbing roses and is also home to many young ferns, especially *Asplenium trichomanes*.

There are two exits from this garden: one is down the stone steps across the central path, which lead to the lower drive, or down onto the croquet lawn at the left of the garden. This is a square lawn, surrounded by balustrades similar to the main garden above. There is a small border on one side and on another a natural rock garden, which, unfortunately, is under some tall limes, not the best of company. There is a small gate in the farther corner of this garden which leads down to the lower drive.

From the formal garden the sound of rushing water can be heard; from the gate of the croquet lawn the noise becomes almost deafening. A few yards down the drive is a bridge from which the cause, a tumbling stream, can be observed. It is a spectacular scene and makes as big a contrast to the formal garden as can be imagined. The water crashes over a series of high waterfalls down

Rydal Hall. As a complete contrast to the adjacent formal garden, a rugged waterfall descends through natural landscape.

through a rocky ravine, under the bridge and continues through high rocky banks of a small wooded garden. The rocky banks are covered with mosses and native flora as well as native trees where they can get a foothold. The little building by the bridge is surprisingly old, having originally been built in 1668–69. It is in fact a grotto, one of the oldest in the country. When the Diocese took over it was in a state of ruin but they have restored it.

The small wooded garden can be approached through a gate on the other side of the drive to the croquet lawn. This is known as the Rockery Garden. It contains two pools linked to the stream above the house, but they are currently in need of repair. This is a pleasant little garden, but as yet, apart from the rocks of the stream's ravine, does little to justify its name.

There is still some way to go in the restoration of the garden. The prospect is an exciting one and doubtless the Diocese would welcome help in any form, but especially in the form of donations and suitable plants. It is not a garden that will take most visitors long to look at, but it is interesting, especially the contrast between the formal garden and the natural ravine. There is no doubt that it also makes a wonderful contrast to the garden of Rydal Mount on the other side of the lane.

Rydal Hall. The sombre formality of the steps leading from the formal garden down to the drive is broken by a line of bright azaleas.

120

25
RYDAL MOUNT
Rydal, near Ambleside

(Owned by Mrs Mary Henderson)

MOST VISITORS who go to the homes of literary figures do so to look at their houses. In some instances, Beatrix Potter's Hill Top (14) for example, they may look at the garden in passing, but it is not an integral part of the visit. For any visitor to Wordsworth's home at Rydal Mount, the garden is as essential as the house, as it was laid out by its owner in a way that fitted in with his deep love of nature that ruled his life and his poetry.

The house had originally been built as a farmhouse around 1550, with further work, including refacing, being carried out on it in the mid eighteenth century. The house was owned by the Le Fleming family who lived just across the lane at Rydal Hall. Wordsworth leased it in 1813 and moved there with his extended family that included his sister Dorothy and his sister-in-law Sara Hutchinson, as well as his wife and three remaining children. They had been happy in the cottage at Grasmere, where they had created a garden (9). Alas, it had proved too small and they had moved to the larger Allan Bank and then to Grasmere Rectory. Unfortunately neither of these proved happy homes. However, the move to Rydal Mount was more successful, much due to the garden, and Wordsworth remained here until he died in 1850.

Apart from the trees having obviously matured, the garden is much as he designed it. It is more formal, at least in the sense of having lawns and paths, than that at Dove Cottage, but the same love of nature dictated its form and its planting. Wordsworth was very interested in gardens and even designed some for his friends.

The first important part of the garden, however, was not Wordsworth's responsibility. Immediately in front of the house is a mound, The Mount, now partly covered in rhododendrons and other shrubs, but still providing a seat with a view; it was originally

Open: *March–Oct, 9.30–5; Nov–Feb, 10–4. Closed Tues in winter and last 3 weeks of Jan. £2 (including house). Gives discount to Dove Cottage (9).*

Directions: *3 km (2 miles) N of Ambleside. Take signposted lane off A591. Limited parking; additional space in lane by church.*

Access: *sloping, but mostly gentle. Paths in wilder part of garden steep and at times slippery.*

Main attractions: *viewing terraces, Dora's daffodil field, bluebell wood and wild area, literary connections.*

Teas: *teashops in Grasmere.*

Plants for sale: *no.*

Nearby gardens: *Rydal Hall (24), Dove Cottage (9).*

used by Norse settlers as a look-out point for raiders from beyond the borders. It was also a signal point, with a beacon lit as a warning of trouble coming along the valley. Wordsworth enjoyed this part of the garden as it gave him views southwards towards the hidden Ambleside and beyond to Lake Windermere, and he would often take tea here.

Back towards the house, the majority of the garden stretches away to the west. A lawn slopes away towards Rydal Water which can just be seen shining through the trees. Above this is a series of terraces which have been fashioned over the natural rock. The Sloping Terrace, which runs along the boundary wall at the very top of the garden, had been partially constructed when Wordsworth took over the house. He finished it and constructed a summer house built against the dry-stone wall. It is difficult now to know what the view was like from here in Wordsworth's day as many of the trees have matured to a great size, blocking the sight lines in several directions. However, glimpses can still be had of Rydal Water and the fells beyond. This is a tranquil spot, and would have been even more so before the constant noise of traffic on the road below. It was a place where Wordsworth spent a lot of time composing his

Rydal Mount. On a typical dull Lakeland day a rhododendron shines out. Two of Wordsworth's terraced walks appear above the rhododendron.

Rydal Mount.
Wordsworth's view of Rydal Water from the summer house at the top of the garden, where he wrote much of his poetry.

poetry. The terrace continues beyond the summer house as the Far Terrace. It is not too difficult to imagine the poet walking to and fro here declaiming to the countryside.

The Sloping Terrace, as its name implies, is quite steep so Wordsworth constructed another one, Isabella's Terrace, that started from the same point, but ran horizontally along the side of the hill. To reach the beginning of each, the visitor must first go up a short flight of stone steps. In Wordsworth's day these housed self-sown yellow *Meconopsis cambrica* — they still do, but the rampant winter heliotrope *Petasites fragans* has also got a hold and has now run through every crack and crevice. There are some magnificent trees planted below Isabella's Terrace which can best be appreciated by walking along that path; one seems to be strolling through the branches of the trees themselves. Amidst the branches of the red acer, one can enjoy the fine tracery and colour of the leaves against the light. Similarly one is able to admire at close hand the fine leaves of the fern-leaved or cut-leaved beech, *Fagus sylvatica* 'Aspleniifolia' (previously *F.s. heterophylla*). At the far end of this terrace, just beyond a very fine *Exochorda*, is the most splendid example of *Enkianthus campanulatus* that one is likely to see. It can be admired from either terrace as its top is well up over the Sloping Terrace by the summer house. Visiting it once after a storm I found the ground inches thick in its bell-shaped flowers.

Beyond the Sloping and Isabella's Terraces is the wilder part of the garden. A stepped path descends from the Far Terrace making its slippery way down past the water garden to the croquet lawn. This end of the garden really is wild with brambles and weeds fighting for control. The path and water garden are, however, in a relatively tamed part, the upper slopes being carpeted with bluebells in spring, just as they were in Wordsworth's day. There is no great gushing stream in the garden as there is in the neighbouring Rydal Hall. Here it is just a trickle of water moving from pool to pool, down a somewhat irregular water course. It is in woodland and is edged with wild flowers, mosses and ferns, many of which have doubtless found their own way there or have survived since they were first introduced by Wordsworth. Further down, its course flattens out creating a large damp area in which grow introduced plants such as *Rodgersia*, *Peltaphyllum* and *Lysichiton*.

At the bottom of the slope the croquet lawn comes as a bit of a surprise as it is a large flat area of mown lawn, seemingly in the middle of a jungle. It has been excavated out of the hillside, with dry-stone retaining walls and banks on two sides, the other two dropping rapidly towards the lake below. In one corner is a stone hut, although it is quite plain it has an element about it of the ginger-bread house hidden in the forest. There is a small terrace here with wonderful views through the beeches to Rydal Water.

A steepish path leads up to the main lawns with views across to the house. In spring the house from here is cradled in rhododendrons, most of which seem likely to have been planted since Wordsworth's time. To the right a path leads down to a gate labelled 'Dora's Field'. This was a paddock which Wordsworth bought for his daughter Dora. On her death he and his wife, Mary, planted many daffodils (supposedly 80 000) in her memory. There is no access to the field, which belongs to the National Trust, from the garden, but it can be visited through the churchyard just down the lane. It is no longer a field, more of a wood as it is full of mature trees but the daffodils still bloom here each year, followed in turn by a great swathe of bluebells, another of the poet's favourite flowers.

The path on the right-hand side of the lawn leads along the bottom of the hill on which the terraces are situated. It is dominated by the same trees which overhang the upper paths and also has more, smaller, acers and rhododendrons backing it. A new feature here which did not exist in Wordsworth's time is the herbaceous border which lines it along its length. This is not a very wide bed, but is well planted with peonies, delphiniums, hostas, nepetas, aruncus and other perennial plants. Towards the house the natural rock is exposed and is delicately populated with self-sown foxgloves (*Digitalis purpurea*). The stepped path that leads back up to the house passes a small rock garden, predominantly covered with heathers.

Before leaving the garden there are a couple more small pleasant terraces and enclosed gardens between the main garden and The Mount for the visitor to explore and perhaps to sit awhile and reflect.

The layout and design of this garden would do much credit to a modern garden designer and it says a lot for Wordsworth's love of nature and interest in gardens that he was able to create something that was to stand the test of time as well as his poetry has.

Rydal Mount.
Wordsworth's house sits amongst contrasting lawns and tree- and shrub-dominated terraces.

26
SELLET HALL

Whittington, near Kirkby Lonsdale

(Owned by Judy and George Gray)

Open: *March–Oct, 10–5; other times by appointment. 70p. Nursery and shop open all year.*

Directions: *just s of Kirkby Lonsdale, off A65. Take Burton-in-Kendal road through Low Biggins and follow signs. Ample parking.*

Access: *mostly level except for knoll. Some steps but wheelchair access to most of garden.*

Main attractions: *herb garden (labelled), ponds and bog garden, herbaceous plantings, young acer plantation.*

Teas: *nice teashop.*

Plants for sale: *attached nursery specializing in herbs and acers.*

Nearby gardens: *Sizergh Castle (27), Levens Hall (19).*

SELLET HALL is slightly out of the normal Lakeland area, but it is well worth making a diversion to see. In fact it lies not far from the M6 at the southern end of the Lakes and thus is just right for the first or last garden visit to this area if you come from the South. It will not be a disappointment, especially if you are interested in herbs or acers.

The garden is quite extensive, covering about 1.4 hectares (3½ acres) on the southern side of the attractive house that has Tudor origins. The garden, however, is of a much more recent date as very little exists from before the present owners came here about twenty years ago.

The Grays' initial garden in 1972 was the large lawn surrounded by shrubs and borders above the house. There followed a whole sequence of gardens as their interest grew in what they were doing, until the present size and layout was reached. These were mainly taken in from the surrounding fields, although this is hard to visualize now as they are mature enough to appear to have been there for centuries.

Each of the seven gardens is a distinct unit and is either surrounded by the original field walls or by newly planted (now mature) hedges, which not only enclose the spaces, but also keep out the strong winds that this part of the country tends to receive.

To many gardeners the most fascinating part is likely to be the herb garden. This is an extensive rectangular area, enclosed by tall yew hedges. It is divided into four sections by two paths, one running down the centre of the garden and the other across it. Where the two meet in the middle is a fountain. The paths are currently lined with rosemary, although this may change, and the two ends of the longer one have an edging of different thymes. Each

Sellet Hall. One of the many gardens is this bog garden filled with interesting, moisture-loving plants.

of the four sections of lawn has a series of variously shaped beds, each filled with several different herbs. The majority are clearly labelled with both their Latin and English names. This is just the place to visit if you want to sort out your thymes and mints, or any other herbs for that matter. As an added bonus most are also available from the nursery that lies just through the hedge. Three small gazebos occupy the position where the paths end against the hedge. These are covered with honeysuckle.

At right angles to the herb garden and running from behind the shop is a narrow garden split into three distinct areas. The first is a terrace and a series of ponds surrounded by a moist area covered with gravel in which astilbes, acers and *Pinus* 'Mugo Mops' grow. This is immediately outside the shop and provides one of the few sitting areas in the garden. The main part of this garden is taken up by four long beds, each surrounded by a low box hedge. Although it does not look it, the ground here is surprisingly moist and it is able to support *Astilbe* 'Sprite', hostas and *Heuchera* 'Palace Purple', laid out as bedding plants, a good example of using plants that suit the conditions. To one side there is a bed of roses including some aged plants of *Rosa glauca* (*R. rubrifolia*) and *R.* 'Canary Bird'.

Below this, the third part is really a separate garden: a bog garden well stocked with moisture-loving plants, such as hostas, sibirica-type irises, candelabra primulas (*P. japonica* and *P. pulverulenta*), the lily-of-the-valley relative *Maianthemum bifolium* and aquilegia. The surprising thing about this garden is that a large clump of *Polygonatum multiflorum* thrives under a big horse chestnut (*Aesculus hippocastanum*) in one corner. This is unusual in that it is virtually impossible to get anything to grow under this type of tree.

Moving next door we find the main garden that runs away from the back of the house towards the horizon. Immediately next to the house is a flagged terrace; the walls are covered with enormous plants of *Clematis montana* which perfume the air in spring. Steps lead down onto the lawn, which is bisected by a central path that is flanked by herbaceous borders. This path seems to disappear towards the distant fells as it ends at a ha-ha. The borders are delightfully planted in white, pink and blue and include such plants as *Anthemis punctata cupaniana*, with white daisies open mainly in the spring, although the silver foliage remains throughout the year. Other plants of interest include *Geranium renardii*, *Dicentra spectabilis alba*, white *Geranium sylvaticum*, *Macleaya*, *Echinops ritro* and several

Sellet Hall. The main herb garden contains several gazebos that are attractively covered with climbing plants.

Papaver. The borders around the edges of the lawn have a mixed planting including other colours. One nice combination is the orange-red *Euphorbia griffithii* 'Fireglow' with yellow *Meconopsis cambrica* growing through it. It is interesting to note that the Welsh poppies in this garden are tinged apricot-pink rather than the usual orange.

Sellet Hall. A beautiful planting with contrasting shapes and colours. The mint forms a fresh background for the allium and linaria.

To one side is a small rose garden with a central pergola over which climbers are trained. This is newly planted, but once mature should make a wonderful intimate garden and it seems a pity that provision has not be made to leave space for a seat so making an opportunity to linger.

Beyond the drive (on which there is a wonderful dark red tree peony, *Paeonia delavayi*) is the upper lawn which was the first part of the modern garden to be created. This is a large sloping area of grass surrounded by borders of shrubs that have been interplanted with herbaceous material. The top of the hill is dominated by a large clump of purple-leaved hazel, *Corylus maxima* 'Purpurea'.

Tucked away behind the shrubs at the top of the lawn, in the shade that they like, are several plantings of double primroses. There are also many other herbaceous plants in this area, surrounding a central mound of *Cortaderia selloana*. Although this is the very top of the garden, moisture-loving plants, *Ligularia przewalskii* for example, still seem to thrive.

129

The bottom border of this garden is devoted to heathers with a few conifers. Just above it is an island bed devoted entirely to dwarf conifers. There is a bigger island bed filled with mature shrubs, with a few herbaceous plants, including *Geranium macrorrhizum album* (which makes a good ground cover) in front of them.

The final garden is back beyond the herb garden. This is a large area consisting of about an acre of rough grass in which grow azaleas and rhododendrons and an interesting collection of acers. All these trees and shrubs are relatively newly planted and are still dominated by mature trees of oak and ash. The land naturally builds up into a knoll on which is placed a pergola. Hidden from view until you have reached the top of this mound is a large pond which has yet to be planted. The grass is generally kept quite long here and wild flowers grow in it including a carpet of bluebells which cover the mound. Paths are mown through the grass so access is easy.

Attached to the garden is a very nice nursery. It is immaculate in the way it has been laid out with neat beds. Perhaps more to the point is the fact that the plants are of excellent quality and at a very reasonable price. The main types of plants for sale are herbs and acers. The former look fresh and appealing and the latter are sturdy plants at prices that are the cheapest you are likely to find in the area for such quality plants. Depending on the season, you will also find other plants for sale such as dwarf conifers and primulas.

As well as the nursery there is also a shop containing herby things, including seed and books, as well as other items such as jams. There is also an attractive café for tea or coffee. In the shop there are photographs of the house and gardens before the present owners started work on them and it is only after seeing these that the full extent of work they have put into them becomes apparent.

Altogether this is a garden well worth visiting. Although relatively recently planted it has an air of maturity about it, partly contributed by the yew hedges, dry-stone walls and the house itself. Carefully chosen vistas between the gardens also help with this feeling. Perhaps it has not got the range of plants that you may see elsewhere, but there are still many to see, especially herbs and acers. Most of these are labelled so it makes it a good place to go to check up on their names; the rest of the garden is not so well labelled (but then this is really a private garden and apart from the two collections mentioned one would not expect to find a forest of labels). As well as the plants and the effect they create, the contrast between the individual gardens and the extensive views make this an enjoyable place to visit.

27
SIZERGH CASTLE
Near Kendal

(Owned by the National Trust)

I<small>N GARDENING</small> terms Sizergh is the biggest and the best of the National Trust properties in Cumbria, not only in conception but also in upkeep. The series of gardens seem to have a logical sequence about them and the planting is not only aesthetically pleasing, but also has much for the plantsman. The herbaceous border, in particular, is one of the best in the Lake District.

Nearly all the larger houses mentioned in this book started life as a pele tower, and Sizergh is no exception. The need for defence was acute in this area near to the Scottish borders from which raids frequently took place. The tower was built in the mid fourteenth century and it is around this that the rest of the house has developed. The majority of the garden was laid out by the Strickland family (residents at Sizergh for 750 years) in 1926 although some elements, such as the border above the main lawn, are of earlier origin.

Although there are two ways into the garden the best is through the rose garden, the entrance of which is just below the ticket office and shop. By going this way round the best elements of the garden are left to last. The first thing that will be noticed if the approach is made in summer is the large stands of tiger lilies by the path under the yews. In the spring there is a nearby clump of *Neillia thibetica* with stems a bit like raspberry canes and lovely spikes of pink flowers. Another plant to see in its full splendour in spring is the *Magnolia* × *soulangiana*. This, like many of the roses, is underplanted with *Geranium macrorrhizum*, which makes one of the best ground covers. *Geranium endressii* is also used for the same purpose here. Other spring-flowering ground-cover plants include the bright blue *Pulmonaria angustifolia azurea* with its bronze edge to the plain leaves, and the over-large form of the lily of the valley, *Convallaria majalis*

Open: *April–Oct, 12.30–5.30 (Castle 1.30–5.30). Closed Fri, Sat. £1.60 (free to NT members).*

Directions: *6 km (3¾ miles) s of Kendal. Entrance on A590 just sw of junction with A591. Ample parking.*

Access: *some steps and slopes, but much can be visited by keeping to level ground.*

Main attractions: *huge rock garden, wild-flower meadow, rose garden, herbaceous borders, spring bulbs, year-round colour.*

Teas: *nearest tearoom at Levens Hall (19).*

Plants for sale: *at Levens Hall (19) and Halecat Nursery (13).*

Nearest gardens: *Levens Hall (19), Halecat (13), Holm Crag (17).*

Sizergh Castle. Part of the long herbaceous border, showing the central section which is particularly endowed with hot colours.

'Fortin's Giant'. In the summer there are plenty of interesting roses and a small *Magnolia liliiflora*. Another plant of the early summer which will have much to offer in years to come is the young handkerchief tree, *Davidia involucrata*. In late summer and autumn, interest is maintained by a *Eucryphia × nymansensis* 'Nymansay'. An avenue of limes used to mark the path of the main entrance to the castle, but these have now gone and have been replaced by young *Sorbus aucuparia* 'Beissneri'.

Pass through the gateway and there is a choice of routes, either along the lower terrace to the right, along to the border to the right at the top of the lawn, or straight across the lawn itself to the castle, the last being the least attractive choice. In fact the entrance to the lower terrace is just before the gateway, via some steps which lead down to a paved area on which there is a summer house, beside which grows a graceful red acer. The summer house looks out onto a sweep of grass that stretches towards the castle. It is separated from the lawn above by a dry-stone retaining wall. This is dotted, but fortunately not overdone, with plants such as wallflowers, aubrieta and the indispensable white daisy *Anthemis punctata cupaniana*. Along the top of the wall is a low hedge of *Fuchsia magellanica gracilis*.

Taking the top route the visitor passes the oldest part of the garden. The end of the terrace is marked by an apsidal summer house, built into the wall. This looks towards the tower past many interesting shrubs and climbing plants. This border must be warm in winter as plants that are considered relatively tender grow well here. A giant phormium, for example, or the incredibly tall *Phygelius capensis* which is flowering 3–3.6 m (10–12 ft) up the wall. Apart from having to crane one's neck to look at the flowers, there is another price to pay and that is that the base is very bare and leggy, requiring something else to be grown in front of it.

The mixture in this border is very much of the familiar and less familiar, with the plants planned to give flowering throughout the seasons. One of the earliest to flower, and perhaps less usual, is the evergreen *Clematis armandii*, while the much more common rosemary flowers on and off for most of the year. Later in the season the

Sizergh Castle. Arum lilies beside one of the pools in the large rock garden, which is famed for its acers and ferns.

various buddlejas bloom, both *B. lindleyana* with its strange pleated flowers and *B. fallowiana* 'Alba' are present, as well as the spectacular Mount Etna broom, *Genista aetnensis*. Many of the shrubs are fragrant such as the delightful, late spring-flowering *Daphne × burkwoodii* 'Somerset'.

At the end of this border the pele tower looms. Its foot is rimmed with *Erigeron karvinskianus* (previously *E. mucronatus*), the Mexican daisy. This plant is indispensable in most gardens as it flowers over such a long period and often in places where little else will grow. It can spread if it is happy, but it is little problem to control. Also, surprisingly, at the foot of the tower is a large spread of *Gentiana acaulis*, not the easiest of gentians to grow, here used almost as a bedding plant. Steps lead from the front of the castle down to the lake. In part this is the remains of the moat, but it has been extended. There is a small island which in mid summer is a blaze of white, with marguerites (*Leucanthemum vulgare*) and meadowsweet (*Filipendula ulmaria*). The parapet on the house side of the lake is swathed with *Clematis montana* for spring flowers and the vine *Vitis coignetiae* for autumn colour. At the far end is an interesting planting of trees including the rarely seen ash, *Fraxinus ornus*. Coming round the end of the lake the visitor joins a path that goes along the bottom of a small sloping field. This is the wild-flower meadow. This includes a good section of wild flowers including at least six species of orchid. Early to mid summer is the time to see this meadow at its best. Later than that, most of the flowers are over, but betony, *Stachys officinalis*, still grows amongst the browning grasses and can look deceptively like an orchid at a quick glance.

The path beside the wild-flower meadow leads back towards the house and round to the side where there is one of the glories of Sizergh, the rock garden. This was constructed and planted in 1926 and is now fully mature, too mature in fact as many of the trees have outgrown their space. These are being replaced and certain areas of rock have been cleared as part of the renovation scheme. No garden is ever static and this type of work must be expected. However, there is still much to see here. The actual layout of the weather-worn limestone rock, with its pools and streamlets is very impressive. The scene is much enhanced by some very fine acers. One of the features of this part of the garden is the number of ferns that are grown. So often rock gardens are associated with plants that dislike moisture and prefer an acute drainage. Here in the Lake District with its high rainfall, moisture-loving plants, such as ferns, do very well and it makes sense to use them in this context. There are many other damp-loving plants, especially in the more shady areas. Plants such as *Rodgersia*, *Astilbe*, *Veratrum*, and *Brunnera* all do very well. As one would expect, the conditions are also ideal for a range of primulas, especially the candelabra types. Not all the rock garden is moist. Towards the north-east the paths lead up amongst the rocks on quite a steep hillside. This is the area that is currently most under renovation and there is not a great deal planted here. However, what there is is more drought tolerant, such as bergenias and these plants are thriving in their new home.

Leaving the rock garden by its northern corner, one comes out onto a lawn on the other side of which is a long herbaceous border. This is obviously mainly a summer feature, but it's also surprisingly effective in spring. The emerging hummocks of the herbaceous plants form a green basis for the border with colour being provided by a number of clumps of both orange and yellow *Fritillaria imperialis*, as well the acid yellow of the freshly opened *Euphorbia polychroma*. There are a few other plants in flower, such as *Pulmonaria saccharata* 'Mrs Moon' and *Helleborus* × *sternii*, which add to the colour. Between them they give an astonishing impression of the border being full.

Come summer, then the border is indeed full. The colour scheme at this time of year seems to pay lip service to Gertrude Jekyll's ideas of hot colours in the centre of the border with paler ones towards the ends. On the whole it works, but there are occasional plantings that seem to interrupt this scheme. For example the planting of the pink and white climbing rose, *Rosa* 'American Pillar', behind the centre of the hot colours, which includes the oranges of *Helenium*, *Ligularia*, *Hemerocallis*, does little for the scheme. However, these are small criticisms as this is generally a beautiful border with many well-grown plants.

Following the path round towards the house, the visitor will pass the orchard, having first passed two *Cercidiphyllum japonicum*, that look especially good in their autumn colour. Here, in spring, are many colourful bulbs flowering in the short grass. The snake's-head fritillary, *Fritillaria meleagris*, is to be seen in profusion as well as bluebells and, unusually in grass, grape hyacinths (*Muscari armeniacum*). Yellow is provided by the much despised dandelion, *Taraxacum officinale*.

The tour of the garden has now been completed as the visitor is entering the courtyard to the house and it is just a short distance back to the cars. It is an interesting garden with much variation in the different areas. There is much to be seen at different times of year and so it can be visited frequently without getting bored, perhaps a good test for a garden.

28
STAGSHAW

Near Ambleside

(Owned by the National Trust)

Open: *April–June, 10–6;
July–Oct by appointment
(contact NT Regional
Office, Grasmere). £1
(free to NT members).*

Directions: *just s of
Ambleside, on A591. Look
for sign on sharp bend (on L
if heading s). Parking
difficult; or park at
Waterhead, 0.8 km (½ mile)
to N, and walk
(partly footpath).*

Access: *hilly, with
narrow, often slippery paths.*

Main attractions:
*rhododendrons, woodland
ground cover, moss garden.*

Teas: *teashops in
Ambleside and Windermere.*

Plants for sale: *no;
nearest garden centre is
Hayes, nearer Ambleside.*

Nearby gardens:
*Brockhole (5),
Holehird (15).*

ON A WET, drizzly, spring afternoon you could easily imagine that you were in the Himalayas as you walk up and down the steep paths amongst rhododendrons and other more unfamiliar plants. On a warm sunny afternoon you could equally imagine that you were in those mountains, but you are more likely to be conscious that you were in the Lake District, with continuous glimpses through the trees of shining Windermere, with its white sails, and the fells beyond.

Although it is hard to imagine, Stagshaw is a relatively new garden. In 1957 the National Trust were left Wansfell House and the estate around it. They did not want to hold onto the house, but were keen to have the land involved. Cubby Acland, already the regional agent for the Trust, rented a couple of the cottages that came with the estate and, seeing the potential of the piece of ground that rose behind them, set about creating a garden from it over the next twenty years.

The land in which he had the vision to see a garden was a strip of steep, rocky woodland that ran up onto the fells. Towards one side, a stream tumbled down its rocky bed, keeping the atmosphere under the trees moist and buoyant. Cubby Acland set about judiciously thinning the wood, creating paths and glades and, above all, planting. Although he planted many other trees and shrubs it is the rhododendrons for which he, and subsequently Stagshaw, became famous. He introduced over 350 different rhododendrons and azaleas to the garden, creating a profusion of colour on the hillside. The colour was far from random and the grouping of the shrubs was carried out with much care. Sometimes, such as in the area of azaleas half-way up the garden, they form a tapestry of colour, at other times a single specimen stands out majestically against the surrounding green trees. Occasionally there are clumps of the same colours, perhaps planted one above the other like a floral waterfall, often with camellias and magnolias joining the tumult. Cubby Acland, alas, is no longer alive to look after the garden, but it still continues as he laid it out, now under the National Trust's care.

The hillside is a myriad of narrow paths, sometimes muddy and often steep; making it a garden only for the fit or those who are prepared to take it slowly. Occasionally they flatten out with resting places, often with wonderful views of Windermere through the trees. Towards the top of the slope the paths cross the busy stream that rushes down the southern side of the garden, filling the trees with the noise of its progress. One of the rocky outcrops towards the top of the garden has been turned into a moss garden, something that can be done in an area of high rainfall.

In spring, when the main attention is focused on the flowering

Stagshaw. This steep fellside garden presents constant, glittering glimpses of Lake Windermere through the trees and shrubs.

trees and shrubs, the ground flora seems almost incidental, with a few clumps of interesting plants, but in the main being restricted to ground cover. Most noticeable amongst the latter is *Maianthemum bifolium*, forming large patches of fresh, shining green with little spikes of white flowers, a little in the manner of their cousins, the lily of the valley. There are other large areas of the native yellow archangel, *Lamium galeobdolon*, with silver splashed leaves and yellow dead-nettle flowers. Like the *Maianthemum*, this is rampant and should only be grown in large gardens or in areas where it can easily be controlled. Here it can roam to its heart's content. Many rhododendrons form ground cover in their own right as they prevent light and moisture reaching the ground beneath them, so little can grow there.

Some of the most spectacular ground plants to be seen are the clumps of dog-tooth violets, *Erythronium*, part way up the southern path. Another group in the middle of the garden are the veratrums, with their wonderful pleated leaves. There are also a few clumps of lilies which add an exotic touch towards the end of spring. Daffodils (*Narcissus*) carpet the ground in places. Towards the house these are often modern hybrids but further into the garden these are replaced by the more typical wild daffodils, *N. pseudonarcissus*. Bluebells, *Hyacinthoides non-scripta*, also cover the ground in sheets with their characteristic colour and perfume. Although it is probably better to have each in its own season, it would be interesting just once to see both the yellow and blue in flower at the same time.

However, interesting as the ground flora is, it is the trees and shrubs that are the main components of this garden. Besides the rhododendrons and azaleas there are many other very note-worthy plants. In the late spring one of the most spectacular is the Chilean fire bush, *Embothrium coccineum*. There are in fact trees, some a good 9 m (30 ft) high, rather than bushes, and there are several in the garden, mainly towards the bottom. Their name is very apt as it looks as though the hillside is ablaze, so intense is the flame-red of the flowers, the leaves being insignificant at this stage. Also in this area are several trees of *Magnolia sinensis*. These are wide spreading, open trees, that always seem to have a peaceful quality about them. The flowers hang down so that you can look up into the white saucers with their red and cream central bosses. These flowers, surrounded by their glossy, bright green leaves, are truly beautiful and, to add to their charms, they are perfumed.

Visiting this garden can be a bit of an adventure, not only because of its resemblance to a Himalayan hillside, but because of the sudden appearance, as you turn a corner, of an unexpected tree or bush. These pleasures are not confined to the summer; later in the year it becomes a blaze of autumn colours with acers and bushes such as *Disanthus cercidifolius* leading the way.

Although this is a woodland garden with everything planted on a large scale, there is one ingenious piece of planting that could be in the smallest of gardens. The box for collecting the entrance fee is built from local stones cemented together. Gaps have been left on the woodland face of it into which *Ramonda myconi* has been planted. These plants prefer a cool north situation, especially if they can be planted on their side so that no water collects in the plant's crown. This is a nice touch for the departing visitor to enjoy.

Stagshaw. The shady reverse of the collecting box showing how even unexpected places can be used effectively for plants, in this case ramonda and sedum.

29
STATION HOUSE
Wright Green, near Lamplugh

(Owned by Mr and Mrs G. Simons)

Open: *under National Gardens Scheme (see Yellow Book).*

Directions: *10 km (6 miles) s of Cockermouth. Signposted when open from A5086 at Cross Gates. Ample parking.*

Access: *level, except for vegetable and herb gardens, approached via steep bank.*

Main attractions: *foliage garden created from old railway line, large vegetable garden, new herb garden.*

Teas: *served in garden. Light lunches available at Barn tearooms, New House Farm, on B5289.*

Plants for sale: *propagations from garden.*

Nearby gardens: *none open at the same time.*

FORTUNATELY no two gardens are alike. The sheer variety of situations, designs and plantings means that garden visitors can pursue their hobby without ever becoming bored. Throughout the country there are several well-known gardens that have been created on the sites of old railway stations, each dealing with the situation in a different way. In Cumbria one such station was at Wright Green, not far from Lamplugh, on the old Workington–Whitehaven line. It was closed in the mid 1960s and five years later the present owners moved into the house.

There is not much left now to tell that there was once a station here, although there is more evidence of a railway line, the most obvious being the bridge across the road by the gate. There is also another bridge some way from the garden in the opposite direction, which forms a focal point down the length of the garden during the winter when there are no leaves on the trees. Another indication is the fact that the garden is linear in shape, along the line of the track, and that it is on top of a very free-draining embankment. A final piece of evidence is the base of the signal box, now used as a sunken garden, with sinks displayed upon it, the box itself having long since disappeared.

Unless you have all these details pointed out to you, it is likely that only the name of the house would make you aware of the original use of this piece of ground. It is not only the provenance of this garden that is different from most others in this book. It is also the plants: the garden is almost totally trees and shrubs, and, for a change, this does not mean rhododendrons and azaleas although there are a few. This then is a green garden, much dependent on the shapes and textures of the leaves, as well as variations in its basic colour, for its attraction. However, this is not to say that there are no flowers in the garden, because, quite naturally, the trees and shrubs all have flowers of some sort, some such as the *Syringa* and *Laburnum* quite prominently so.

The drive past the house leads through the oldest part of the garden, one of the oldest inhabitants being a large multistemmed laburnum. It is a very floriferous form with long racemes of flowers. One of the first things that was added to the garden was a shelter belt beside the position of one of the old sidings. This not only provided shelter from the wind, but also a certain amount of shade and it was along here that the Simons decided to place their rhododendrons, again some of the original plants in the garden. Walking along the line of the old sidings leads naturally to the main part of the garden, the old railway line itself. Apart from a large area of planting towards the middle of the garden, this is mainly linearly planted, along the margins of the track. This track has been sown with grass and is now a long elegant lawn.

At the north end of the lawn is a curved apse of conifers. Within this is a rose garden which is suffering badly from the attentions of rabbits. Rabbits and the occasional deer are the scourge of many gardens in the Lakes. The only real solution is to put a small meshed netting all round the garden, but this is an expensive and no mean task in a large garden.

The trees and shrubs are not exceptionally rare, but are interesting and well displayed. There is little duplication, although there are two tulip trees, *Liriodendron tulipifera*, magnolia relatives. One of the most dominant trees is the variegated poplar, *Populus* x *candicans* 'Aurora'. The leaves of this fresh-looking tree are splashed with white and touches of pink and constantly moving. It has the characteristic smell of balsam in the spring. Another variegated tree is a sycamore, *Acer pseudoplatanus* 'Leopoldii' with yellow to lime green splashed on the leaves.

It is important to look closely at the plantings as there are often interesting items tucked away. For example there is a young maidenhair tree, *Ginkgo biloba* with its curious fan-like leaves. It is a plant that is extinct in the wild although fortunately it is relatively common in cultivation. When buying a plant of this it is best if you can acquire a male plant as the fallen nuts from a female plant have a somewhat unpleasant odour should the tree manage to bear any. It comes from China, whereas *Ribes odoratum* comes from central North America. This in many respects is similar to the flowering currant, *Ribes sanguineum*, except that the flowers are yellow. A curiosity that seems to be much in demand by flower arrangers is the fasciated willow, *Salix udensis* 'Sekka' (previously *S. sachalinensis*

'Sekka'). There are many conifers dotted around the garden, which help to bring colour and texture during the winter. However, with so many trees and shrubs about there is plenty of interesting structure and bark to be seen.

There are a few herbaceous plants about, namely a group at the end of a lawn behind the house, planted mainly with blue, yellow and white. Plants here include *Aruncus dioica*, *Helenium* 'Butterpat', *Lysimachia punctata*, *Campanula lactiflora*, delphiniums and *Alstroemeria aurantiaca.*

At the bottom of the railway embankment is a large vegetable garden, something not frequently seen in the gardens in these parts. A new herb garden is also being developed on this lower level.

This, then, is a simple garden, almost entirely devoted to trees and shrubs, but one worth visiting.

Station House. One of the most striking trees in this garden is the variegated poplar *Populus × candicans* 'Aurora'.

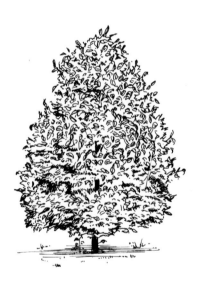

30
UNDERFIELD

Greenodd, near Ulverston

(Owned by Mrs D. P. Dickson)

IT IS ALWAYS a joy when one unexpectedly comes across a garden open to the public and such a one is Underfield. It is not listed in any directory of gardens, but there is a notice on each of its two gates announcing that it is open, giving the charity for which is donating the gate money for that day.

This is a private garden on the southern edge of the Lakes not far from the sea. This helps to keep it warm and one of the glories of the garden is a plant that requires this protection from cold. This is the Chilean fire bush, *Embothrium coccineum*, which here is growing as a small tree. In early summer it is absolutely ablaze with its flame-red flowers. Alas, in spite of the Gulf Stream it is still not warm enough for the humming birds which normally pollinate it.

Apart from this tree the main attraction of the garden is the wonderful display of rhododendrons and azaleas. In spring you are immediately conscious of them as soon as you enter the garden, they seem to be everywhere. The best view of them is from the lawn in front of the house, from where much of the garden can be seen. Close by, bordering onto the grass are dwarf members of the genus, further away they develop into large rolling clouds of flowers.

Taking the path from the right of the main lawn the visitor joins the stream on its way to the lower garden. Growing in the supporting walls to the path there is pennywort, *Umbilicus rupestris* with its shining round leaves and spikes of tubular brown flowers. This is not a common plant in the Lake District, it is more a plant of the walls and banks of south-west England. Beside the stream are bold clumps of Solomon's seal, *Polygonatum × hybridum* that love this kind of cool moist situation. Also here are clumps of the summer snowflake, *Leucojum aestivum*.

Once in the lower garden the most noticeable thing is the banks

Open: at owner's discretion (check for Open sign on gates). £1.

Directions: 6.5 km (4 miles) N of Ulverston. 1.5 km (1 mile) N of Greenodd on A590 look for gate on L (unmarked except for Open sign). Second entrance via lane leading from Spark Bridge. Small car park near house.

Access: on several levels but slopes mostly gentle.

Main attractions: rhododendrons, sunken glasshouse, duck pond, bluebells, monkey puzzle stand.

Teas: not available locally.

Plants for sale: a few. Nearest nursery is Next Ness, near Ulverston (see Nursery chapter).

Nearby gardens: Holker Hall (16).

of rhododendrons and acers that dominate the scene. The rhododendrons do not all open at once, giving a sequence from spring through into summer. Facing the rhododendron bank and below the lawn that runs from the front of the house is a terrace leading to a sunken glasshouse. The gardener must descend some steps to enter, the only piece of the structure above ground being the sloping glazed roof. The advantage of this type of house, which with mass production has unfortunately gone out of favour, is that they require little heating. The ground acts as a massive storage heater, slowly releasing its heat and preventing the ingress of frost.

The terrace is backed by herbaceous plants including *Hemerocallis* and *Cephalaria gigantea*. Below the terrace is a wall containing a fig tree, *Hibiscus syriacus* 'Jeanne d'Arc' and a *Callistemon citrinus*, all again indicating the warmth in this south-facing garden. Below the terrace is a lawn, another greenhouse, a large vegetable plot, an unusual sight in this part of the world, and several fruit trees. Beyond these is a pond with several varieties of duck.

There is a path leading round the bottom of the pond and

Underfield.
Rhododendrons and azaleas, sometimes contrasted with swathes of bluebells, make this a garden well worth visiting in spring.

Underfield. A sunken greenhouse in which only the glazed area is above ground. This type of structure will often remain frost free without heating.

through a gate to a wilder part of the garden. This is a journey well worth taking in late spring as there is a large area of grass and emerging bracken that is full of bluebells. If this were not a sight in itself the area is surrounded by yellow azaleas, *Rhododendron luteum*. Not only is the combination of so much blue and yellow marvellous, but also the combined scents are incredible. This garden has much to offer, yet it is worth coming for this alone. This area is quite extensive and there has been some new plantings, especially of monkey puzzle trees, *Araucaria araucana*. This is a wise foresight as these are quite dominant trees in the garden and since some are obviously mature there is always the threat that they may one day blow over. There are two main clumps of these spreading conifers with their wrinkled grey bark, one at each of the gateway ends of the two drives. They are magnificent specimens and there are enough of them to form quite large stands.

The paths from the bluebells and azaleas lead back to the drive not far from the embothrium. Opposite is a shrubby honeysuckle and under the shrubs a delightful double wood anemone, *Anemone nemorosa* 'Alba Plena'. There are many other interesting trees and shrubs to look at as well as herbaceous plants in this garden.

It is worth a diversion to see this lovely garden. Spring is perhaps its best time but there is sufficient of interest to make it worth visiting at any time.

The Natural Garden

Possibly more than any other part of the country the Lake District has a wild flora that is accessible. There has been little development nor any widespread use of herbicides on roadside verges to reduce the native population. Many odd corners have been left to nature's own devices and, of course, there are vast tracts of upland that are not only unspoiled, but often easily accessible to the visitor who wants to see plants growing in their wild habitat.

Throughout these areas there is a great diversity of flowering plants from maritime ones of the coast and estuaries to the smaller alpine plants of the upper fells. The amazing thing about many of these plants is that they are either ancestors of, or at least related to, our garden plants and are easily recognizable as such.

Of all these plants it is probably the water plants, which are seen everywhere in the Lake District, that will be the most familiar. Early in the season the banks of streams and lakes are yellow with the kingcup, *Caltha palustris*, at the same time complemented with drifts of the lilac of the milkmaid or cuckoo flower, *Cardamine pratensis*. Both of these are known in the garden, especially in their double forms. Another common lover of damp areas, frequently seen in the garden, is *Persicaria bistorta*, bistort. In cultivation the flower spike is always much more substantial than in the wild. Later, in the summer there are the tall purple spikes of the purple loosestrife, *Lythrum salicaria*, of which there are many improved forms in cultivation. Alongside the roads and in boggy areas one frequently comes across great swathes of the frothy cream flowers of the meadowsweet, *Filipendula ulmaria*. An attractive plant of such areas also commonly seen in gardens is the yellow flag iris, *Iris pseudacorus*. Another yellow is the yellow loosestrife, either *Lysimachia vulgaris*, the wild form, or *Lysimachia punctata*, which is commonly found as a garden escape.

The stream and lake banks are often so richly clothed in colourful plants that they look like herbaceous borders. The roadside verges are just as abundantly supplied. One of the most exciting sights, especially for people from further south, is that of *Geranium pratense*. In places the roads seem to be entirely lined with its light purple flowers. Earlier in the year the same roads may well be white with sweet cicely, *Myrrhis odorata*, a herb frequently seen in gardens. Water avens, *Geum rivale*, frequently grows by the roadside and is a familiar sight for most gardeners with its nodding pink flowers. In the late spring and early summer the roadside verges in some areas become yellow with cowslips, *Primula veris*. In other parts of the country these have become almost extinct but they still exist here in quantities.

One roadside surprise for visitors is the ubiquitous, but delightful, Welsh poppy, *Meconopsis cambrica*, which flowers everywhere in this area, not only in the wild but also in most gardens, self-sowing happily, sometimes too happily as it can become a pest in spite of its beauty. In the Lakes it is nearly always seen in its

The natural garden. A natural 'border' of meadowsweet and yellow loosestrife growing beside a beck running into Coniston Water.

The natural garden. A wide range of wildflowers that are as attractive as any garden border.

yellow form, whereas further south it often occurs in gardens with an orange flower as well. It seems to be especially fond of growing in or at the base of dry-stone walls.

Walls would make a fascinating study in this area, so many plants seem to like them, perhaps because of their free-draining nature in what can be a wet climate. As well as the meconopsis they are home to the red valerian, *Centranthus ruber*, although it is mainly near habitation or by the sea where it is normally seen. Ferns are great denizens of walls and can be seen in profusion all over the Lake District; they love the moist atmosphere.

The undisturbed nature of the country is good for some of the rarer plants, and orchids in particular can be found in various places. Early purple (*Orchis mascula*) and spotted (*Dactylorhiza fuchsii*) orchids are the most frequently seen, even by the roadside. There are several more to be seen, especially in the damper areas, including the unspectacular bog orchid *Hammarbya paludosa*. A little more noteworthy is the broad helleborine, *Epipactis helleborine*, which is occasionally found in woods.

Woodlands provide a number of plants that are familiar in gardens. The cool Solomon's seals, *Polygonatum* × *hybridum* and *P. odoratum* can be seen. In some, the lily of the valley, *Convallaria majalis*, is well established, although it is doubtful whether these are native plants. Campions, *Silene dioica*, light up many a woodland glade and it will come as no surprise that bluebells, *Hyacinthoides non-scripta*, often clothe the ground in coppices and woods. These look and smell magnificent in the wild but can be a nuisance in the garden. Never a nuisance is the primrose, *Primula vulgaris*; one can never see too many of them. These still occur in large numbers in light woodland and on field banks throughout the lakes.

If one plant characterizes the Lake District then it must be the wild daffodil, *Narcissus pseudonarcissus*. This is seen in vast quantities, both in semi-wild and wild conditions. Its cheerful yellow flowers set against the Lakeland's lush spring greenery are a sight to behold and one well worth going to the Lake District just to see. Although there are acres of meadowland covered with them they are just as much at home in light woodland. The vast conifer forests, however, that cover parts of the fells are very sterile and are hardly worth visiting for wild flowers although they may well offer other aspects of wild life.

However, Grizedale Forest is certainly worth visiting, not only for the forest and its contents, but also because it has an area of nursery beds that the public can wander around. Also in this old walled garden are a number of the trees that the visitor is likely to meet in the forest, which have been labelled with their names. There is also a sales area where a number of these trees can be purchased. They are still small, not much bigger than seedlings, and so will easily fit in the boot of a car — there will be no need to drive around for the rest of the holiday with a tree sticking out of the roof. The tracks through the forest and up to the open moorland are well marked and have a good surface, although some paths can be a bit steep.

Up in the hills it is more difficult to find wild plants, although they certainly exist. The conditions are much harsher here and so plants either adapt or take advantage of any shelter they can find. The plants are usually short and grow close to the ground in the short turf. Here thymes, dwarf potentillas and the smaller bedstraws, *Galium*, grow. Plants often grow in the crevices of rocks, not only as a protection from the incessant wind but also to avoid grazing. This is particularly noticeable in areas of limestone pavements. Here it is very interesting to look down into the fissures to see what is growing there. Surprises can await. For example the wood anemone, *Anemone nemorosa*, will often be found here, finding amongst the rocks the protection and shade that it would otherwise get in woods, but here well above the existing tree line. Perhaps they are relics of when the area was forested at some distant time in history. A diminutive relative of the garden lady's mantle, *Alchemilla mollis*, can frequently be found on higher ground, and

The natural garden.
Wildflowers abound throughout the Lakes. Here a patch of cowslips adorn a roadside bank near Sizergh Castle.

often lower down as well. This is *A. alpina*, the alpine lady's mantle.

The beauty of the Lake District is that nearly all these plants, with the possible exception of the mountain flowers, can be seen alongside the road, no special expedition need be mounted; even the car-bound are able to see them. 'See' is the operative word, for by all means look and photograph them, but do not remove them. All are available from nurseries, often in much better forms, and under no circumstances should they be dug up. The Lakes is one of the remaining havens for wild flowers and it should be allowed to continue as such. If you want a memento of your holidays either take pictures or go to some of the local nurseries and get something that is much more likely to be of benefit to your garden. It is sad to relate that most plants dug up from the wild, especially by people on holiday, rarely survive the journey home, let alone live to see another flowering season in the garden.

When searching for wild flowers, never forget to have a look round any churchyard that you come across. They are a haven for all kinds of interesting plants, even orchids if you are lucky. They do not have to be unkempt to be of interest, indeed those that are mown two or three times a year are likely to be more productive.

Wild flowers can bring as much pleasure, if not more, than their cultivated counterparts. They do need more effort to find them, but it is usually well worth while.

NURSERIES

GARDENERS visiting an area are rarely satisfied with taking home just pleasant memories and ideas, they are also often very keen to have a look at what plants are for sale and perhaps take home some treasure that they have been seeking for a long time. To them nurseries become almost as important as the gardens. Many of the gardens have plants for sale and in many of the private ones the gardener is often willing to propagate a plant by special request (a donation for the charity that they are collecting for is a suitable response to this kind offer).

The Lake District is not terribly rich in nurseries, but there are enough interesting ones scattered around to make it worth while seeking them out. Many garden centres have people to give advice, but they rarely have time to chat about plants. On the whole specialist nurseries are more plant orientated (they rarely sell sundries such as toilet roll holders) and they are usually run on a shoe string by people who are plant enthusiasts. Next to growing plants they like to talk about them (and a late third is actually selling the plants). Much information and advice can be obtained from such people and many a happy hour can be spent in their company — but do remember that they have a living to earn, so do not outstay your welcome.

These old-fashioned nurseries normally have a good range of basic plants plus a few unusual ones and one of the joys of such places is to discover, often tucked away, a plant that has been long sought. These nurseries are not as clinical as garden centres and you must be prepared, in some cases, to find a few weeds around. They are also not so well staffed so do not fret if you to have to wait to be served on a busy day.

There are several good garden centres in the Lake District, all carrying a wide range of plants and in some cases unusual ones. They are more business-like with quite a different pace of life. Although they obviously sell plants they also carry a wide range of sundries, in some cases items that seem to bear no relationship to gardens at all, but if you prefer this type of shopping then there is ample opportunity to enjoy it. The plants are generally of a good quality, although some that are left at the end of the season are often flagging through lack of attention other than watering. They can also be horribly root-bound so avoid buying anything in a pot that is obviously distorted by the thrusting roots. In spite of denials on their part they are not always accurate on plant names and it is not unusual for a pot to be wrongly labelled, so always look at the plant as well as the label when buying. However the labels for each section are generally quite informative and for the beginner who is shy to ask questions most garden centres can provide many of the basic plants that are required.

Unfortunately because of their vast overheads their plants are usually more expensive than those from a nursery; in some cases within the Lakeland area the price of plants can vary as much as four times between a garden centre and a nursery. This brief review has generally put the garden centres at a disadvantage, as far as the plantsman-gardener is concerned, but they can still be worth a visit, particularly as many are widening the choice of stock they offer and unusual plants can now be found at many. Frequently they also stock a good range of gardening books, often a better selection than can be found in local bookshops, and with the demise of the ironmonger-garden store they may also have the best stocks of fertilizers, tools and other sundries.

There are one or two old-fashioned nurseries dotted around. The most famous of these is Reg Kaye's Waithman Nurseries at Silverdale, Carnforth, just to the south of the Lakes. He founded it in 1930 and it quickly became a mecca for anyone looking for alpines, ferns or unusual plants. The nursery is now but a shadow of its former self, but brave efforts are being made to bring it back to life. For those who are used to the clinical surroundings of a garden centre this nursery may come as a bit of a shock, as it says in the introduction to the catalogue '. . . an old friend remarked that finding plants here was like searching for them in their natural habitat'. Do not let this deter you: there are some very interesting plants to be found and at very reasonable prices.

Rock garden plants still take up quite a large area of the nursery and it still contains the best selection in this part of the world. Ferns was one of Reg Kaye's great interests (in 1968 he published a standard work on the subject and this is currently being revised) and a large selection can still be found at the nursery. Ferns are grown in many of the Lakeland gardens and for anyone with cool, shady conditions they are invaluable. The only problem with them is that they can become addictive as many gardeners have found out. In spite of there not being as many varieties on offer as in former times the nursery still provides a happy hunting ground for both beginners and addicts alike.

Although alpines and ferns represent the main interest of the nursery there are still very large collections of herbaceous perennials, including hostas, and shrubs. Some of the latter, such as *Cornus* 'Norman Haddon', are rather difficult to find through garden centres. Again the prices are quite reasonable. There are stocks of plants beyond the public's gaze so do not hesitate to ask if there is something that you specifically want; indeed do not hesitate to raise any problem as the staff are well informed and very friendly. An informative catalogue of their stock is available (60p in 1991). It is shut on Sunday mornings and at weekends in the winter. A lot of words have been spent on this nursery but it is one of the most important and best loved in the area.

Another old-fashioned nursery is that of T. H. Barker and Son, Baines Paddock, near Haverthwaite. This may not be of the same stature as Kaye's perhaps, but none the less one well worth visiting. It is not far from Holker Hall and makes a good addition to a visit to those gardens. Although it grows a few bedding plants it is mainly concerned with herbaceous perennials and shrubs and is slowly building up a good stock. Clematis is its main speciality and they are currently propagating over 200 varieties. Needless to say with such a range they include several that are unusual and it is well worth visiting the nursery for these alone. The prices are reasonably cheap and the plants well grown. Like so many of the smaller nurseries in the Lake District the owners are passionately interested in plants and are only too willing to talk about them.

A third old-fashioned nursery is that of Halecat at Witherslack. This is probably the main nursery for herbaceous plants in the Lakes. It has a large stock of both common and less common plants. They carry quite a number of the plants that are regularly seen in the Lake District, including some of the moisture-loving ones, such as *Rodgersia, Aruncus* and *Astilbe*. There is also a good stock of hostas. It has a fine array of *Geranium, Euphorbia, Artemisia, Iris* and many other herbaceous plants. If it is said to specialize in anything, it must be in hydrangeas, of which it has an excellent collection. If you have spotted one at Holehird which you especially like, then Halecat may be able to provide you with a plant. Many of the perennials and shrubs that are available can be seen in the adjacent gardens (see page 65). The prices are very reasonable and there is a catalogue. They are closed on Saturdays and Sunday mornings.

Yet another old-fashioned and friendly nursery, although its appearance is a bit more modern (i.e. a bit tidier), is that of Next Ness Nursery. This is tucked away in the lanes of Next Ness, just north of Ulverston, but it is well worth seeking out. Although it has a reasonable number of shrubs and roses, it is for its herbaceous plants that it is to be most commended. It has a very good selection of top class plants, many of them slightly out of the usual. For example it has five or six varieties of *Platycodon grandiflorus*, including double, white and pink forms. They also have some interesting *Aquilegia* of the Vervaeneana group. As well as plants for the herbaceous border there is also a good selection for the herb garden, including such plants as the marshmallow, *Althea officinalis*. The plants are well grown and well cared for. Those that need shade are stored under plastic netting and not allowed to scorch as in many garden centres. The plants in the sales area look so colourful in the summer that it resembles an herbaceous border. This is a very pleasant nursery to visit and doubtless one that will grow in importance. Anyone visiting the south Lakeland area should drop in and see it. The prices of the plants are very reasonable. Unfortunately they do not produce a catalogue.

If it is herbs or acers that attract attention then a visit to the nursery attached to Sellet Hall gardens (see directions p. 126) is well worth a visit. It is not far from junction 36 on the M1 so it makes a good place for a final stop for those making their way south after a holiday or short visit. It has a coffee shop to help make it a break. This is a very well laid-out nursery with neat beds and everything clearly labelled. The plants are well grown and the acers, always a costly item, relatively cheap. Besides these two there is also a good selection of dwarf conifers and primulas as well as hostas and other plants. All can be seen growing in the gardens that are open to the public.

Further north Larch Cottage Nursery, Melkinthorpe, a few miles south of Penrith, is a mixture between a garden centre and a nursery. It has a fairly basic stock of plants although there are one or two plants, such as *Anemone sylvestris*, which are bit more unusual. Unfortunately it is on the pricey side (by way of example *Potentilla aurea* 'Aurantica', an attractive and not that common a plant, being nearly four times the price of those being sold elsewhere in the

Lakes, in a more traditional nursery). However, it is worth looking at for the odd unusual plant. There is a Japanese garden at the bottom of the nursery that is in the process of being established and there are other display beds around the edge of the nursery. There is a very nice tearoom with homemade cakes.

There are a number of garden centres dotted around Cumbria. Most are pretty run of the mill with little to excite the visitor who will probably find much the same plants as in his local one. However there are one or two worthy of mention.

Hayes, on the southern outskirts of Ambleside, has become a bit of a legend, not only in the Lake District, but also much further afield. This reputation is justified as it is doubtless one of the best garden centres in the country. Even if you are not keen on this type of gardening establishment it is still well worth a look. The plants are always immaculate, with many in flower, forming drifts of colour across the sales area. Naturally they have a fairly basic stock of plants, but there are also quite a number of rarities. Some are not so rare or rarer than they state. For example the *Roscoea humeana* they had on display in summer 1992 were nearly all *R. cautleoides*, a much more common plant (although still not that frequently seen

Next Ness Nursery. The rows of potted plants in the sales area give the impression of a colourful border.

155

in garden centres), with the exception of a few plants which were the much rarer hybrid *R*. 'Beesiana'. There was not a *R. humeana* in sight. The nearby *R. cautleiodes* were labelled correctly. This question of naming is a nightmare for garden centres, more so than for nurseries who tend to grow their own stock. Hayes is fortunate in having very good enquiry service for customers, but errors still creep in. As well as a very good selection of herbaceous plants, including such things as *Helleborus multifidus*, *H. cyclophyllus*, *Salvia argentea* and several meconopsis, there is a very good selection of alpines. For example they stock five different *Cassiope*, some of the larger pots containing excellent plants. There are also such unusual plants as *Polygonatum hookeri*, *Anemone ranunculoides*, *A. nemorosa* 'Allenii', and *Dodecatheon pulchellum* (*D. pauciflora*), as well as good pots of *Gentiana verna*, and *Ourisia* 'Snowflake'.

The big disadvantage of Hayes is their prices, which are on the high side especially when compared with those of the traditional nursery, which have only a fraction of the overheads of such a large organization. Also the pricing must seen strange to a plantsman, with, for example, the ubiquitous self-sower *Alchemilla mollis* costing nearly three times the price of the relatively rare and quite difficult to propagate *Linum* 'Gemmell's Hybrid', of which Hayes have a wonderful stock.

There are a lot of other things here besides plants including cheap wet-weather gear for those caught in the rain. There is also a café (two if the weather is fine) for tea, coffee and light lunches. There are also extensive demonstration plantings, the one behind the alpine area being especially good.

There is another large garden centre not that far away in Kendal (in the north of the town at Burnside Road, clearly signed from the main road). This is Clarence Webb, a wonderful rambling old nursery, the sloping floors of the covered area vying with the surrounding fells in their unevenness. It too has quite a large good basic stock with the occasional unusual plants such as *Anemone obtusiloba*. There are occasional problems with names. *Epimedium youngiana* 'Rosea' had labels stapled to the pots declaring that they were *E. versicolor* 'Sulphurea', in spite of the obvious difference in colour. Almost next door a batch of *Euphorbia griffithii* 'Fireglow' was labelled as *E. cyparissias*. They have a good selection of shrubs, in particular rhododendrons and azaleas. There is a coffee shop that also serves light lunches. The prices seem to be slightly down on Hayes.

Most of the other garden centres in the Lakes are pretty routine with little that cannot be purchased at home. Beetham Nurseries on the A6 just south of Milnthorpe is a rather nice one with a selection of good quality plants. Unfortunately the majority seem to come from Blooms which means, for visitors at least, that they can be bought anywhere in the country, but still, this may be a centre worth visiting if you are passing.

One so-called garden centre is Stanley Mossop's Boonwood Garden Centre at Gosforth, near Seascale, but it seems, in truth, more like an old-fashioned nursery. They specialize in some of the more exotic house plants and in particular achimenes. They have the biggest selection in the country and although they have to be bought by mail order it is worth calling into the glasshouses at the nursery to see what varieties are available. If you want a memento of the Lakes the perhaps this is the place to go as many of their own varieties are named after individual lakes such as 'Coniston Water' or 'Grasmere'. They produce a detailed catalogue.

Many of the gardens also sell plants, some with just a small stall, others with a full-sized nursery. Sellett Hall and Halecat have already been mentioned, but there are others such as Lingholm and Muncaster.

Garden plants are often just a bit more than a pretty flower; they are often imbued with all kinds of memories, sometimes of the friend that gave it, or sometimes of the place where it was bought. There is always room for an extra plant in the boot of the car even if it means throwing out a suitcase.

INDEX

Page numbers in *italic* refer to the illustrations